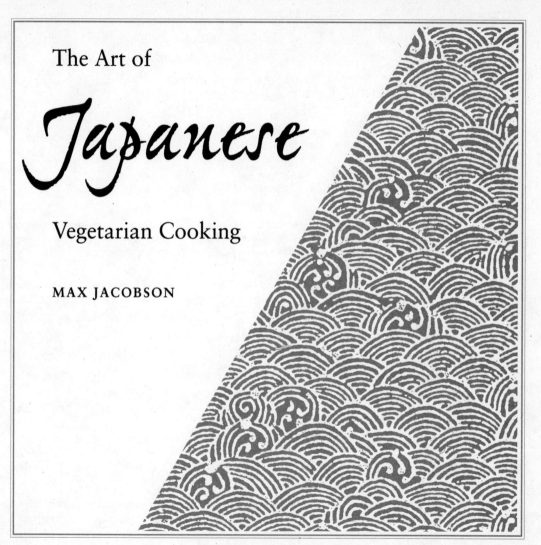

The Art of

Japanese

Vegetarian Cooking

MAX JACOBSON

PRIMA PUBLISHING

Prima and colophon are trademarks of Prima Publishing, a Division of Prima Communications, Inc.

Library of Congress Cataloging-in-Publication Data

Jacobson, Max, 1949–
    The art of Japanese vegetarian cooking / by Max Jacobson.
      p.   cm.
    Includes index.
    ISBN 0-7615-0308-0
    1. Vegetarian cookery.   2. Cookery, Japanese.   I. Title.
TX837.J13   1996
641.5'636'0952—dc20   96-3805
                                            CIP

96 97 98 99 00 AA 10 9 8 7 6 5 4 3 2 1

Printed in the United States of America

HOW TO ORDER:
Single copies may be ordered from Prima Publishing, P.O. Box 1260BK, Rocklin, CA 95677; telephone (916) 632-4400. Quantity discounts are also available. On your letterhead include information concerning the intended use of the books and the number of books you wish to purchase.

Table of Contents

Acknowledgments

I would like to thank the many people who helped me with this project; without their assistance this work would have been far less substantial.

American chefs Octavio Becerra of Pinot Bistro in Los Angeles; Charlie Trotter from his Chicago restaurant of the same name; and Mitchell Frieder of Trilogy Restaurant in Los Angeles and Cakes and Company in Lancaster, California, were kind enough to contribute flashes of their own brilliance. Japanese friends and kitchen professionals Hiroshi Serizawa, Ryo Sato, Kozo Terajima, Kimiko Jadibi, Koji Yoshida, and Itsuki-san all provided me with recipe ideas and technical help. Michiko Soffer gave me a hand with Japanese language material, some of which was especially hard to understand.

I owe a debt of gratitude to the Japanese National Tourist Office and particularly to Mr. Hideki Tomioka, who provided me with valuable guidance and helped arrange my last visit to Japan. Hats off to the Takeda family of Ebisu Market in Huntington Beach, particularly Joe Takeda, for taking the time to explain the differences in quality between various types of Japanese products.

And kudos to my colleague at the *Los Angeles Times,* Charles Perry, whose meticulous editorial assistance has helped me enormously in my efforts as a writer. Ruth Reichl of the *New York Times* had sufficient faith in my abilities to steer me on a career path I've both benefited from and enjoyed. Food writer and eccentric-at-large Linda Burum has been a good friend and dining companion.

Huge thanks to my friend and literary agent extraordinaire Wendy Zhorne, who suggested the idea of a Japanese vegetarian cookbook and found me this project.

Finally, I wish to thank my Japanese friends and family, Yoko Makino-Reed, living proof that a macrobiotic diet makes a person beautiful; Hiroko-san, a good mother and a good cook; and most of all Hiroko's daughter, Keiko Yoshimochi-Jacobson. Without Keiko-san's thoughtful psychological insight, clear vision of her native culture, highly developed palate, and infinite patience, I could not have even begun to understand the mystery and complexity that is modern Japan, much less the cooking.

Introduction

*Deru kui ga
utareru*

*The nail that
sticks up gets
hammered
down*

THIS BOOK DESCRIBES not only how the Japanese cook with vegetables, but also explores Japan itself. The Japanese say that one cannot understand a country without understanding its cooking. The axiom rings especially true for Japan, a nation consisting of a group of islands with an unusual culture. Japan is a place filled with rewards, but only for those willing to put in considerable time and energy.

When I first stepped on Japanese soil, I knew virtually nothing about the country outside of what I had learned at the movies: Godzilla, Sessue Hayakawa in *Bridge on the River Kwai,* and Toshiro Mifune's sword-wielding samurai. That changed in 1978 when I arrived in Kobe, a city in the Kansai region later to be devastated by an earthquake. I was on a three-day leave from a job on the *Royal Viking Star,* a passenger ship temporarily docked in the city's port.

Almost from the beginning, Japan's exotic charms swept me off my feet. Kobe then was a lantern-filled city with labyrinthine streets and rainbow colors. Wooden structures and neon signs were everywhere, and every second building seemed to be a restaurant or food stand. I was instantly hooked.

Several years later while living and working in northern California, I met a Tokyo native. (She persuaded me to return to Japan with her in 1983, and we married a short time later.) Alas, the Japan I first visited is mostly a memory now. In the process of the most massive economic recovery in world history, the Japanese have modernized their country relentlessly, razing traditional Japanese *machi* (towns within larger cities) and erecting glass and steel high rises in their place.

Some cities have preserved a few of their old neighborhoods. *Shitamachi* (downtown) in Tokyo comprises districts such as Kanda, Ueno, and Asakusa—

places that retain some old world charm. Parts of Kyoto, too, have been kept relatively intact despite the construction of the monstrous Kyoto Hotel, which blocks access, and even views, to many of the city's landmark temples. In fact, old neighborhoods are still scattered around Japan today. But they are a vanishing breed. Japanese cities are mazes of neon, asphalt, and cold steel. Only in between the skyscrapers is one likely to find a lone wooden house, defiant, the last remnant of a unique culture.

Japan, in fact, is a country fast losing touch with its traditions. One of these is its cuisine. As Japan is now a rich country, its people no longer are constrained by nature's hardships, or the restrictions that severe climate once placed on the diet. Japan enjoys the world's longest life expectancy, more than eighty-two years for women, seventy-nine for men. Gerontologists credit the Japanese diet, which is rich in soy protein, seaweed, raw vegetables, tubers, roots, and grains. It remains to be seen if the average life expectancy will decline now that Western foods have become part of the Japanese diet.

Some claim the Japanese have abandoned their native diet. Walk down any Japanese city street, and you will see American fast food, Western-style bakeries, Chinese noodle houses, and usually a supermarket, where cuts of meat, powdered sauces, flavor enhancers, and premixed foods make Japanese and Western cooking a convenience for the homemaker.

Predictably, Japan's youth have embraced America's obsession with the hamburger. Today, Japanese love beef. But until the Meiji era (the late nineteenth century), it was unknown in Japan. Before that, Japanese living near the coast ate fish (a more efficient way to ingest protein). Inland Japanese foraged, hunted wild boar and deer, and even ate insects such as crickets and grasshoppers.

The Japanese traditionally have eaten a natural foods diet, and so the idea of vegetarian cooking is built in to the cuisine. But because Japanese people have never had an excess of protein until this generation, movements toward strict vegetarianism have come only recently.

Yet Japan has a great Buddhist tradition—and so a historical predilection for vegetarian foods such as tofu, tubers, pickles, and rice. In the eleventh century, Buddhism spread throughout Japan, bringing *shojin-ryori,* an elaborate vegetarian cooking style, along with it. Later, in the Edo period, 1600–1861, the court cuisine in Kyoto (then called Heian-kyo, the "Capital of Peace and Tranquillity") became heavily Buddhist. This Buddhist-influenced cooking survives today in the form of several elegant temple restaurants (for example, Izusen, which is included in the restaurant listings at the end of this introduction).

But it would not be accurate to say that Japanese vegetarian cooking has been a mainstay at any time. In general, Japanese recipes call for a stock called *dashi* as the base for flavoring almost everything they eat, from tofu to noodles to vegetables. Most *dashi* contains three basic ingredients: *kombu* (dried kelp), dried shiitake mushrooms, and *katsuobushi* (dried bonito flakes). The strict vegetarian would not think of consuming this stock, much less cooking with it, since bonito is a fish in the tuna family. But to most Japanese, eliminating the *katsuobushi* from the basic stock recipe fundamentally changes the flavor.

For this book, I have included two recipes for *dashi,* one purely vegetarian and a more traditional one that uses *katsuobushi.* The purely vegetarian stock I have developed employs toasted rice and soy beans and takes time to prepare; it must be well reduced to bring out an intense flavor. I'm confident it will please strict vegetarians and nonvegetarians alike. My vegan friends tell me their taste buds are different from those who eat meat and fish. Natural flavors become more pronounced for them, I'm told, and flavor enhancers such as flaked, dried fish are utterly unnecessary.

In Japan, being a vegan—one who consumes no meat, fish, dairy, or eggs—is very difficult. Most vegetarian restaurants in Japan include fish in their definition of vegetarianism, and that goes for virtually every dish served. Even in a number of Buddhist temples, where eggs are shunned, a bit of dried fish is used to flavor stock.

One of my Japanese friends from Tokyo, Yoko Makino, is a vegan now living in Nimbin, Australia, a place residents of New South Wales proclaim to be the new alternative-lifestyles capital of the world. Yoko is a talented home cook who can make even the simplest vegetable preparations sing. She flavors her stock with Plantaforce, a concentrated vegetable bouillon made by a Swiss company called Bioforce. (The U.S. distributor for this product is Bioforce of America, LTD, Kinderhook, NY, 12106.) One more possibility for flavoring *dashi* is Vecon Vegetable Stock (Modern Health Products, LTD, Gloucester, England). I find both products work well, but both put a distinctly non-Japanese cast on whatever is prepared.

For those who plan on visiting Japan in the near future, remember that most restaurants include fish in their meals. Some temples and restaurants, however, offer a variety of vegan and Buddhist dishes. Many types of sushi, such as *nori-maki* and *kuppamaki*, are naturally vegetarian, and it is common to find them as well as *onigiri* (rice seasoned with pickles and wrapped in seaweed) in local markets. Keep in mind that in most Japanese markets in North America, as well as in any food shop in Japan, some of the sushi and *onigiri* are made with fish stock. If the rice is a bright white color, however, there is a good chance it conforms to vegetarian standards.

A few Japanese restaurants in the U.S. serve vegetarian dishes, but ask in advance to ensure that the *dashi* isn't made with fish. As to Japanese vegetarian restaurants in Japan, I haven't found one yet. Here is a short list of true vegetarian restaurants in Japan.

Tokyo

Bodaiju in Roppongi This is perhaps the best-known vegetarian restaurant in Japan.
Transcendence Perfection Beyond #401 2–2–10 Shimouna, Setagaya.

Kyoto

Izusen located in the Daitoku-ji, one of Kyoto's loveliest temples. Here is where one of the world's most beautiful, yet inexpensive, lunches is served.
Koan located on the grounds of Shotekin Temple, Fukuchi-cho, Nanzenji.
Sujata's Indian Restaurant 87–28 Nishimachi Kitashirakawa.
Unkai in the ANA Hotel Kyoto, near Nijo Castle. This is the best restaurant on the list. They serve a wonderful, yet expensive, eight- to ten-course *shojin-ryori.*

While natural foods and natural foods restaurants are a growing phenomenon in Japan, no purely Japanese restaurant is strictly vegetarian. On a recent trip to Japan, I purchased a book called *Naturareru Restoran Gaido*—"Japlish" for "Natural Restaurant Guide." Unfortunately, the book is written almost entirely in Japanese, except for the addresses and phone numbers. But if you can find a copy, you will get an idea of how many of these restaurants exist today.

I hope my book will satisfy the need for natural and vegetarian Japanese recipes. And I hope you will be encouraged to cook Japanese dishes in your own kitchen. The majority of the recipes are simple, and many rely on soy, sake, sugar, and mirin for their character. Simplicity is the essence of Japanese cooking, and the natural tastes of the ingredients are paramount.

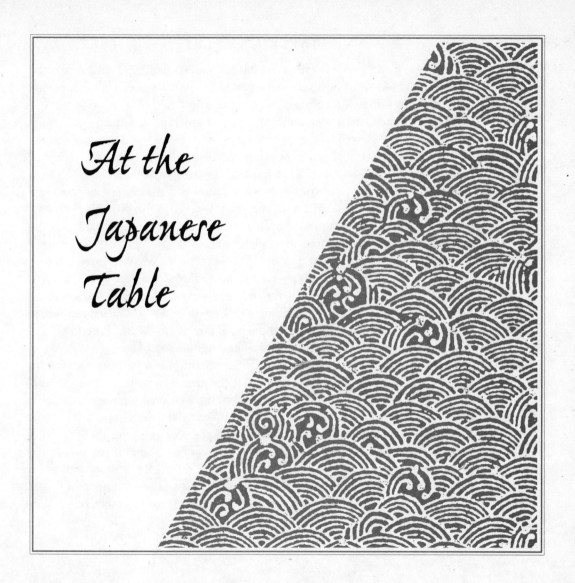

At the
Japanese
Table

Jishin
kaminari
kaji oyaji

Earthquake,
thunderbolt,
fire, father

L IKE ENGLAND, JAPAN is an island nation that takes etiquette with great seriousness. If you live on an island, you've got to get along with others—there's no place to escape to if you don't.

Good table manners are an important part of any Japanese meal, and certain rules should be followed. For example, many of us know that slurping noodles, which creates a ghastly sound, is not only acceptable, but polite, in the right circumstance. That's only one difference from Western standards.

Another difference is a primacy on eating food while it's hot, subordinating the Western custom of waiting until everyone is served. When you are served in a Japanese home or restaurant, simply call out *itadakimasu* ("I'm eating") and dig in. No one will fix you with any baleful stares.

Posture is a very important part of Japanese etiquette. My wife often intoned *shisei ga warui* ("bad posture") anytime I sat in an overly relaxed manner in her parent's home. When eating, raise the food to the lips, rather than bring the entire bowl to them. That is a real no-no, truly *gehin* (low-class) behavior. When sipping clear soups, though, bringing the bowl directly to the lips is perfectly acceptable, providing it is done in a discreet and noiseless manner.

Japanese pickles are formally served in a separate dish with its own set of chopsticks. Use those chopsticks to transfer the pickles to your own dish before you eat them. When eating rice out of a bowl, the well-bred Japanese will finish the very last grain before asking for *o-kawari* (seconds).

When using chopsticks, be careful not to spear foods or use them to drag dishes toward you. Do not wave them around over the food as if you are trying to decide which morsel to attack next. Pour only as much soy sauce into your saucer as you are going to use, and when you finish eating out of anything with a lid, replace the lid as you found it. Now, you're ready for high society.

MEALS

Just as formal Western meals have a specific order, the proverbial soup to nuts, so do most Japanese meals. Yet it's also true that the Japanese are a nation of snackers. Their time-honored tradition of eating small portions—and lots of them—is undoubtedly a factor in their tendency not to store much excess fat, as opposed to the less metabolically efficient habit of feast or famine eating.

A few Japanese meals, such as the *bento* (lunch box), are arrangements of different foods served at the same time, as at a Western picnic. In contrast, most *kaiseki* (multicourse meals) begin with *zensai* (appetizers) and then proceed through a series of courses such as *sunomono* (vinegared foods), *agemono* (fried foods), *yakimono* (broiled foods), rice, pickles, and perhaps some fruit or sorbet. One type of soup starts a meal, others come in the middle, still others, especially those with rice, come toward the end. The order of these courses is rarely, if ever, transposed. One never eats fried foods after broiled, for instance, and almost every Japanese meal ends with rice and pickles.

Many Japanese people eat the main meal of the day at lunch to sustain them through the end of a long work day. Consequently, Japanese lunches are huge. *Teishoku,* or a set lunch, business lunch, or complete meal, is usually the best deal going—a way to eat in a fancy restaurant at a rock-bottom price. Often, a meal that costs twelve hundred yen at lunch, or twelve dollars, might be nearly one hundred dollars during the evening, and more if accompanied by alcoholic beverages.

Most Japanese restaurants, in Japan and abroad, serve *teishoku* and change their menus every day. The meal usually includes some kind of meat, fish, or seafood; rice; miso soup; a small salad; and often coffee or tea. Other dishes commonly eaten for lunch are noodles and *donburi* (one-bowl dishes). Noodles and *donburi* are cheap and filling, and typically cost under ten dollars, even under five on occasion. The *shokudo* is a fast, convenient restaurant, sort of a Japanese cafeteria, that serves both Western and Japanese foods.

Tsukemono

Tsukemono (pickles) are an essential part of the Japanese diet, and a serving of rice and pickles alone is considered a complete, though humble, meal. Originally, *tsukemono* were probably a clever way of preserving vegetables. Eggplants, turnips, cucumbers, red peppers, and practically anything else that grows are used. Some are pickled in salt, others in a paste made from rice bran. Most *tsukemono* are crunchy, and as the well-known writer and Japan observer Donald Richie said, this makes pickles—after noodles, which are slurped—the second noisiest of all Japanese foods.

The most common pickle is called *takuan,* made from daikon radish, which has been fermented with rice bran in a wooden barrel. *Umeboshi,* called a plum but really more of an apricot, is another common variety. Hundreds, even thousands, of Japanese pickles are available. If you are invited into a Japanese home, you can be sure that the family will have their own special pickle recipe. I've never been in a Japanese home where that was not the case.

Should you decide to explore *tsukemono* more exhaustively, I suggest picking up an excellent book called *The Well-Flavored Vegetable* by Eri Yamaguchi, published by Kodansha.

SEASONAL EATING

Seasonality is essential to Japanese cuisine. In the U.S., where *nabemono* (one-pot dishes) are eaten year-round in Japanese restaurants, and tomatoes are ripened with ethylene gas while being trucked to the local supermarket, we seem to have lost this idea. But in Japan, order and *wa* (harmony) according to the seasons are of enduring importance.

In spring, the bitter leafy vegetables, bamboo shoots, and *sansai* (wild mountain vegetables such as fern and dropwort) are eaten. Summer is the time for slurping cold noodles, for eggplant, soybeans, and cool grated vegetable garnishes. Fall, in many ways the most bountiful and beautiful of Japanese seasons, brings mushrooms, including the rare *matsutake;* chestnuts; potatoes; and local fruits. In winter, families huddle in their living rooms, boiling hot pots and eating stews along with lots of radish and plenty of pickles. The American penchant for crossing such seasonal culinary borders violates Japanese sensibilities. To most Japanese, eating *sukiyaki* in the summer makes about as much sense as ordering a hot toddy by the pool in Kapalua.

The Japanese Pantry

*T*HE ASTUTE JAPANESE home cook has a kitchen filled with ingredients and cookware quite unfamiliar to Western cooks: bags of dried mushrooms, a wavy knife designed for cutting tofu, bottled sauces, and long chopsticks for cooking.

There are no substitutes for the flavors of certain ingredients and that necessitates a small investment. If you do not live close by a Japanese market, check the market list at the back of the book for the one nearest you; most will accept mail orders.

Cookware and dishware are also parts of the equation. Many Japanese dishes are prepared in bamboo steamers and cast-iron skillets. Some are cooked in delicate ceramic vessels, which add both texture and a lovely aesthetic to the cooking process, as well as artistic flair. Every great Japanese restaurant has a wealth of the lovely Japanese pottery known as *yakimono*. It is prohibitively expensive—up to one thousand dollars per piece in top-producing cities such as Hagi in Yamaguchi-ken. Each restaurant employs an array of seasonal dishes designed to stimulate the eye and this pottery plays an integral part.

Japanese people admire Limoges china and the beautiful service plates from Villeroy and Boch, but if everything is served on them, you may hear disdain expressed. "Western tables are always set with the same china regardless of the season," I've heard some Japanese say. It's evident that the cultivated Japanese aesthete considers that concept as boring as a bowl of cold oatmeal.

The sky's the limit if you are inclined to spend money on traditional Japanese cookware, utensils, and dishware. I am not in that group. I keep a few necessities: a good rice cooker, a sturdy pair of cooking chopsticks, one durable cast-iron skillet, a sharp vegetable knife, a small set of lacquered soup bowls with lids, and a nice tea set. Any Japanese market sells these inexpensive Japanese items for the kitchen. Or you can, of course, prepare the recipes that follow using Western utensils and then serve them on Western dishware.

BASIC INGREDIENTS

Many Western markets now carry the essential ingredients required to prepare a Japanese meal, but a greater selection is available at an Asian or Japanese market. Furthermore, one can't expect the local supermarket to carry a wide selection of seaweeds. While at an Asian market, stock up on Japanese vegetables such as burdock root, Japanese eggplant, Chinese cabbage, and Japanese cucumbers; you sometimes may have difficulty finding them at your local supermarket.

But whatever you are able to purchase at an Asian market, here are the basics you'll need for the recipes that follow.

Ginger is used in many ways in Japanese cuisine: sliced and boiled for simmered dishes, vinegared and red for sushi and rice dishes, or sweet ginger, a garnish for just about anything. Most Asian markets sell ginger root, or *shoga* in Japanese. Pick ginger as you would carrots; they should be firm, not flaccid.

Japanese rice is short-grained, starchy, and healthful, even though purists in search of more bran may prefer rice in its natural brown state. In Tohoku, Honshu's northern province, the purity of the rice is said to produce the most beautiful complexions in Japan. Much of the best U.S.–grown Japanese-style rice is from Texas and is sold under the brand names Calrose and Tokyo Rose.

Kombu is a form of kelp or seaweed, known as sea tangle in English. *Kombu* is one of the two critical ingredients in *dashi,* the basic stock that good home cooks use to make Japanese food. It is sold in hard dried strips, which must be softened in water before using. When kept dry, *kombu* has a virtually indefinite shelf life.

Kuzu is a high-quality, rather expensive starch used like arrowroot or gelatin as a thickening agent for sauces. Sold in crumbly, white lumps, it is often used as a medicine in Japan. The *kuzu* plant grows wild in many parts of the U.S. and *kuzu* powder can be easily prepared at home. For details see *The Book of Kuzu,* published by Happiness Press, Magalia, California.

Menrui is an umbrella term for noodles, which are a most versatile tool for easy, fast meals. The Japanese love noodles in any form—*soba* (buckwheat noodles); *kishimen* (flat, ribbonlike wheat noodles), which are prominent in Tokyo; *udon* (thick noodles), which are favored at *yatai* (food stalls); *somen* (pure white, thin noodles), which are delicious in cold summer recipes; and *ramen,* the Chinese-style wheat noodles that are consumed in garlicky broths with hearty toppings.

Mirin or *aji-no-mirin,* as it is known in Japan, is a sweet rice cooking wine with a low alcohol content that evaporates during the cooking process. Many of the Westernized Japanese dishes such as teriyaki and sukiyaki use mirin liberally. In Japan's Kansai region where Kyoto, Kobe, and Osaka lie, foods that tend to be richer and sweeter often attribute this characteristic to nothing more than an extra hit of mirin.

Miso is fermented soybean paste. Like similar American institutions such as peanut butter, it comes in myriad forms: yellow, red, white, mixed with sake, and various others. Miso is sold now in supermarkets, usually in twelve- to sixteen-ounce plastic packages. Any Japanese market will offer several choices, but I recommend the full-flavored red and the more subtly flavored yellow miso as starting points. When refrigerated, a good miso lasts for months.

Nori is dried laver (the English word perhaps unfamiliar to all but the most dedicated botanist), a crunchy, delicious hand-rolled seaweed. Sold in diaphanous sheets, it is available at health food stores and Asian markets. Japanese people eat *nori* crumbled up in their miso soup for breakfast, hold sticky clumps of cooked rice with it, use it as the casing for sushi, and crush it for a savory topping on hot foods.

Pan-ko are finely minced Japanese-style bread crumbs that are not really an essential ingredient but are a boon to light and casual frying. They are used to coat foods prepared in the style known as *kushi-katsu* (fried delicacies on skewers). Their name is derived from *pan,* Portuguese for bread, plus the *-ko* suffix used in most Japanese girls' names, meaning "sweet little." Available in Japanese and Asian markets.

Ponzu is a slightly thick soy dipping sauce that gets its distinctive flavor from *yuzu,* a Japanese citrus fruit with a medicinal, limelike taste. If *yuzu* were readily available in the West, one could make a good *ponzu* at home. But it is highly convenient to buy *ponzu* already prepared. The Nakano Vinegar Co. makes a particularly good one.

Rice vinegar is a pale yellow, astringent liquid, called *su* or *osu* in Japanese, and is essential in the preparation of *tsukemono* (pickles), salad dressings, *aemono* (mixed foods), and *nimono* (simmered foods). A reliable brand is Mitsukan.

Sake is a Japanese rice wine used often in steaming, simmering, and braising. Any commercial brand will do, but the ones intended for cooking are less expensive than those intended for drinking.

Sesame oil is used in salads, frying, and marinades. Its nutty flavor is so strong that the oil is almost always diluted, most notably with peanut oil for frying and with rice vinegar for marinating.

Sesame seeds are an essentially Japanese flavor. Ground, whole, or raw, they add texture and flavor to some of the more bland Japanese dishes. *Shirogoma* is the Japanese name for white sesame seeds, and *kurogoma* for black ones. Sesame seeds are delicate and will turn rancid if stored for too long.

Shichimi is one of the few zesty condiments outside of ginger and horseradish in common use in Japanese kitchens. Most markets sell the product in tiny shakers, and it is ideal for flavoring soups, egg dishes, cold noodles, and anything broiled. Translated literally as "seven spices," the components are red chili pepper, sesame seed, poppy seed, dried orange zest, *nori, shiso* (Japanese basil), and *sansho* powder, made from the dried pod of the prickly ash plant. The chili pepper is the main ingredient, and the one that provides most of the heat.

Shiitake mushrooms are the rich-tasting fresh or dried mushrooms frequently used in Japanese cooking. The dried mushrooms should be reconstituted in water for about 30 minutes before cooking. Without them, a distinctive Japanese taste is unobtainable. Shiitake mushrooms are the key to a good vegetarian *dashi*. They are used sliced in soups, minced into rice casseroles, and shaved on egg dishes.

Soy sauce is the salty fermented liquid that is the cornerstone of Japanese cooking. As this is not a natural foods cookbook, I do not suggest using tamari soy to flavor Japanese dishes, although it could serve as a substitute. In my kitchen, I keep a bottle of Kikkoman Extra Fancy Whole-Bean Soy Sauce, a dark soy sauce which is a product of Japan. This inexpensive ingredient is liquid gold for Japanese recipes, an intensely flavored soy that is far superior to the more commercial, more salty, and less complex brands. At times, a recipe may call for light soy sauce. Light soy isn't substantially different from dark in flavor or saltiness. Light soy sauce, however, allows certain vivid colors, particularly those of vegetables, to come through, where a dark soy sauce may darken the vegetables—an aesthetic minus.

Tofu is a neutral-flavored soybean curd that usually comes in large cubes, which are sold water-packed in plastic containers. Tofu is delicate and best eaten while very fresh. Recently voted the food Americans fear most, it is, however, also lionized as a health food. Tofu has both benefits and eccentricities, and is so vital a part of Japanese vegetarian cooking it merits a separate chapter in this book. Many different brands of tofu exist. For the most part, tofu is available in two basic varieties: firm, or *momein* ("cotton"), and silken, or *kinugoshi* ("silk").

Umeboshi is a salty, fermented fruit that has erroneously been called a plum (*ume* is the Japanese word for plum), but it is actually more of an apricot. It is used to add sourness and pungency to bland dishes such as rice porridge or to season the filling in *onigiri*. *Umeboshi* are said to have curative properties: they purify the blood and aid digestion.

Wakame is a dried seaweed that is not for the fainthearted—its tiny, hard black curls look like wood shavings. It may be one of the strangest looking of all ingredients for the Japanese kitchen, but there is no substitute for its rich essence. *Wakame* is used primarily as a garnish, but its powerful presence is also integrated into rice, noodle, and simmered dishes.

Wasabi is the powerful green horseradish generally found in powdered form and then reconstituted in water to make a paste. Many people will not even consider eating their sushi without a snuff-sized pinch of *wasabi*—and a little goes a very long way. A few Asian markets sell *wasabi* in tubes, ready to be squeezed out, like toothpaste.

KITCHEN TOOLS AND SERVING DISHES

Japanese cooking utensils and dishware have changed over the centuries as recipes became more demanding. In general, they are lovely in appearance and highly practical. Without the use of the special Japanese dishes, plates, vessels, and cups designed specifically for some of their recipes, any Japanese meal or dish loses some natural color. The Japanese have a saying, "Western cooking— so many of the dishes are round." (This form of subtle disparagement is interesting, coming as it does from a nation of people who have barely ever questioned the notion that their children be educated in school uniforms, and where employees of major companies virtually are forced to wear suits in the same color and style as their boss.)

Nonetheless, they have a point. The Japanese aesthetic favors asymmetry, and so the idea of putting a round edible in a round dish is a thudding bore to anyone with half an imagination. This is why one sees so many geometric and unusual shapes in Japanese tableware, as they better complement the shape of the food that is placed inside. In the hands of serious cooks or hosts, dishware is as important to the meal as the taste of the food. Japanese food has to be pleasing to the eye as well as to the palate. Interesting tableware is one way the effect is achieved.

Western cooking utensils will work when preparing most Japanese recipes, but it is my belief that the flavors will be subtly altered if that is done. The texture of a vegetable that results from the use of a Japanese grater, for instance, will not be quite the same as that when a Western grater is used. *Oroshi* (grated vegetable garnishes) made to dissolve magically in dipping sauces, will not resemble their counterparts made in a purely Japanese kitchen; they will be rougher, less like pure snow in texture. Using a food processor or blender instead of a *suribachi* certainly can save time, but you give up authenticity—and a good deal of taste, according to Japanese gourmets.

Chawan is Japanese for "tea bowl." They can be made of different materials, from porcelain to lacquerware. They generally are available with covers and are small enough to fit into the palm of the hand.

Chopsticks are the utensils necessary to make eating Japanese food an authentic experience. The Japanese drove me to distraction when I lived there. Every time I ate in public, I heard *o-joozu desu ne* ("My, you are adept at eating with those things"). They were surprised to see a foreigner with the manual dexterity to grasp what they consider an intrinsically Japanese skill. (Probably forgetting the one billion Chinese with equal dexterity.)

The truth is somewhat less earth-shattering. Chopsticks are quite easy to use, and they make any Japanese meal feel, and even taste, more real. *Hashi,* as they are called in Japanese, or *waribashi,* the throwaway wooden chopsticks that come in little paper pouches, require a little practice but really no more so than holding a pencil. The long, beautiful, and formal lacquered chopsticks that may be set out in a Japanese home are slightly harder to use than their wooden cousins, but the technique is the same.

Grasp them about three-quarters of the way toward the wide ends. Hold one in the crook between your thumb and index finger, with the shaft resting motionless against the first joint of the ring finger. Now hold the top chopstick in a scissorlike grip between the index and middle fingers, supporting the shaft with the tip of the thumb. You'll be picking up sesame seeds in no time. Just relax and remember, do not grip the chopsticks toward the tops, or narrow ends. Not only is that considered vulgar in polite Japanese society, it is less functional as well.

Graters are useful for preparing vegetable garnishes. A Japanese grater can be bought for about three dollars. An inexpensive model is a plastic box with a hard plastic grater top. As you run vegetables (generally radish, carrot, or ginger) over the grater, the gratings conveniently fall into the box.

Hocho or *bocho-Hocho* means "knife," the Japanese cook's most prized utensil. No self-respecting sushi-maker would dream of letting another use his; a good knife is more personal than a toothbrush. Traditional Japanese knives are handmade from tempered steel, sometimes by renowned swordmakers. You can pay hundreds of dollars for a handcrafted knife. But I recommend using a stainless steel *usubabocho,* a flat-bladed knife that you'll find for about twenty dollars at most large Japanese markets. It's also a good idea to get a tofu *bocho,* which is under five dollars. It has a six-inch blade, which is rippled like a ridged potato chip.

Kobachi are large bowls used for ramen, noodles, stews, and *donburi.* They are inexpensive and come in a variety of designs.

Makisu are small woven straw or bamboo mats used to roll up sushi or in a Japanese-style place setting.

Nabe is an all-purpose Japanese word meaning either pot or pan. *Nabe* are the first things a good Japanese cook needs. *Donabe* are earthenware pots used in the preparation of one-pot dishes such as *nimono.* They must not be placed directly on a flame when wet, lest they crack. *Sukiyaki nabe* refers to a heavy, long-handled cast-iron skillet that often comes with a round wooden cover with a wooden handle running across the middle. When the Japanese fry, they often use a conventional wok. But light frying can be done in a Japanese-style frying pan, which is usually cast-iron with a wooden handle.

Otoshi-buta is a wooden cover with a handle down the center that can be placed directly atop foods when they are cooking in a pot. Because it is made of wood, it will not crush fragile foods such as vegetables as they simmer. It also keeps foods moist while cooking and allows their flavors to circulate back into whatever is being cooked.

Rectangular omelet pan is a small metal pan used for making *tamagoyaki* (flaky Japanese omelets). If you want to splurge, forget the nonstick pans available and buy the copper ones.

Rice cookers make the cooking process virtually foolproof. I invested about seventy dollars in a good rice cooker, and the investment has paid handsome dividends. Reliable manufacturers include Panasonic, Farberware, and, for the ultimate in price and quality, Zojirushi.

Shamoji is a large wooden spoon used for serving rice.

Suribachi is an indispensable Japanese version of the mortar, which was once made of stone but now usually is made of earthenware. It is used to grind, purée, mash, and blend. The long wooden bat called *surikogi* is its pestle. Traditionally, the *surikogi* is crafted from fragrant cedar, a wood the Japanese associate with autumn.

Dashi and
Miso—
Soups

PUNGENT SCENT IN THE alleyways of any major Japanese city is that of *dashi,* the basic soup stock that flavors virtually every Japanese dish. *Dashi* is what gives most Japanese dishes their characteristic flavor. It traditionally is prepared with *kombu* (dried kelp), dried shiitake mushrooms, and *katsuobushi* (dried bonito flakes), which adds a fishy, penetrating flavor.

Because this is a vegetarian cookbook, such a stock would be inappropriate. My version of *dashi* uses *kombu,* soybeans, roasted rice, and shiitake mushrooms. The rice and soybeans are an innovation—without them, the *dashi* would not have a very complex or smoky flavor.

In my view, sometimes a vegetable dish benefits from bonito-based stock to keep it from seeming overly bland. But most of the recipes in the book that use vegetarian *dashi* are also well-seasoned; they call for salt, sugar, soy sauce, mirin, and occasionally *aji-no-moto* (MSG), though its use is optional. MSG has been demonized by the media, but recent studies have shown it to cause no harm, especially in the minuscule quantities recommended in a few of the recipes.

For variety, I am including a second *dashi* recipe, which is bonito-based. Those who aren't absolute about their vegetarianism may find that this *dashi* improves the flavor of some of these dishes. Even some Buddhist temples in Japan that call themselves vegetarian use a fish-based *dashi.* In protein-poor Japan, the masses never felt the same impulse toward strict vegetarianism, as many in the West have. The vegetarian tradition in Japan, such as it is, has evolved slowly. It has never caught on with any degree of popularity until recently.

Whichever *dashi* you choose to prepare, be aware of its delicacy. No chef or home cook would keep a homemade *dashi* around for much more than a day. After a day, the stock loses pungency, aroma, and freshness, and should be thrown away. The long soaking process the vegetarian *dashi* requires makes it strong and flavorful. A stock relying on bonito flakes requires considerably less time to acquire its characteristic taste.

- Use this as a base for soups, as a simmering or steaming liquid, or simply to flavor sauces and stews.

7 ounces dried *kombu*
2 quarts water
4 ounces dried soybeans
1 ounce Japanese rice
2 ounces dried shiitake mushrooms

Soak the *kombu* in the water for about 6 hours in a large pot.

In a dry cast-iron skillet, lightly toast the rice and soybeans over a low flame, until the rice is golden brown and the soybeans glisten. Add the soybeans, toasted rice, and shiitake mushrooms to the pot with the *kombu* and bring to a slow boil. As soon as the water starts to boil, remove the *kombu*. (Leaving the *kombu* in while boiling may cause the stock to become bitter.) Cover, and simmer on the lowest heat possible, for up to 12 hours, or overnight.

Pour the stock through a strainer lined with cheesecloth or any thin cloth.

Standard Dashi

- 6 ounces *kombu*
- 2 quarts water
- 1 1/2 cups *katsuobushi* (dried bonito flakes)
- 1 tablespoon whole-bean soy sauce
- 1 tablespoon salt

Makes about 2 quarts

Place the *kombu* and the water in a large pot and bring to a rapid boil. As soon as the water comes to a boil, remove the *kombu*. Add the *katsuobushi* and remove the pan from the heat. Allow to steep for 5 to 7 minutes. (The longer you steep the *katsuobushi*, the fishier it will be.) Pour the *dashi* through a strainer lined with cheesecloth. Stir in the soy sauce and salt, and the *dashi* is ready to use.

• Miso soup is served every morning for breakfast all over Japan and is often embellished with seasonal vegetables, tofu cubes, radish chunks, and whatever else the home cook feels like adding. Most office workers wouldn't dream of starting a day without it, and everyone from farmers to business executives partake. In a country where fried eggs and Mister Donut have largely replaced the traditional Japanese breakfast, this nutritious staple remains a constant. But miso soup often performs its magic at the other end of the day as well. It is often the last thing tired workers eat at their favorite *izakaya* (pub), before padding off down the road home, or catching the last train to the faraway suburbs.

Usually sold as a thick paste vacuum-packed in plastic, miso is available in dozens of varieties in the U.S. In Japan, hundreds are available—a wondrous assortment often varying only slightly in texture, flavor, and color from region to region, like a yield of fine vineyard grapes. I use the affectionate colloquial name, *o-mi-o-tsuke,* for the next recipe instead of the more common *misoshiru.*

• *Shiro miso* (white miso) is mild and low in salt; varieties of *akamiso* (red miso), on the other hand, are very salty and have a stronger fragrance. Miso soups typically rely on the flavor of their particular *dashi* for character. But a great variety of vegetables may be added to enhance miso soup: bite-sized squares or triangles of Chinese cabbage; finely chopped lettuce; sliced green onions, leeks, mushrooms, or okra; thinly sliced butternut squash or sweet potatoes; whole snow pea pods; cut green beans; rounds of daikon; bean sprouts; cubes of tofu; *wakame* (seaweed); even minced *natto* beans. Among the few vegetables not recommended are green pepper and celery, which have strong flavors that tend to clash with the delicate perfume of miso.

> 4 cups water
> 1 cup *dashi*
> 8 ounces silken tofu, cut into $^1/_2$-inch cubes
> 4 fresh shiitake mushrooms, sliced
> 3 to 4 tablespoons miso, or to taste
> 2 green onions, chopped

Bring the water and dashi to a boil in a pot. Add the tofu and mushrooms, reduce the heat, and simmer gently for about 3 minutes. Add the miso and stir to dissolve completely. Immediately turn off the heat and add the green onions. Do not overcook the soup after adding the miso as it will weaken the flavor.

NOTE: Feel free to add vegetables of your choice, but remember to cook the hard vegetables longer. If you are using a combination, add the soft vegetables after the hard vegetables have cooked partially.

Suimono are clear soups that bring out the essence of whatever is visible under the surface. All of the great Japanese chefs prepare *suimono* with artistry, and perhaps no other medium in Japanese cuisine is as exquisite, personal, or illustrative of the differences between East and West.

Suimono

•

*Clear Soup
with Tofu,
Onion, and
Cucumber*

Serves 4

    8 ounces silken tofu, cut into 8 equal cubes
    1 quart *dashi*
    1/2 small cucumber, peeled, seeded, and cut into thin slices
    2 spring onions, peeled and halved

Place the tofu gently into a pot and add the *dashi,* bringing it to a slow simmer over low heat. Place equal portions of cucumber and onion into Japanese lacquered soup bowls. Carefully transfer equal portions of the tofu to the bowls as well. Pour the hot *dashi* over the tofu and vegetables, filling each bowl to the brim.

Gohan—
Rice

Bath, rice,

sleep, and

come here

(allegedly the

only words a

traditional

northern

Japanese

farmer speaks

to his wife)

CONTROVERSY EXISTS AS TO the proper way to cook rice, the staple of the Japanese diet. I'm going to offer two ways, one using a rice cooker and one using an old-fashioned, ordinary pot.

Rice is more than just food to the Japanese—it is wealth, health, and prosperity rolled into one. In feudal times, *samurai* were paid in it. A proper Japanese meal is unthinkable without it. Today, traditional Japanese families still eat rice at every meal: for breakfast, with seaweed, pickles, and a raw egg; for lunch, with curry sauce, fried with vegetables, or in sushi; for a snack, in *onigiri* or bite-sized sushi forms; at dinner, plain surrounded by a series of savory dishes.

- 2 cups Japanese rice
  2 1/2 cups cold water

Rinse the rice in the cold water in a large bowl for a minute or two, using your hands as a sieve. The water will become slightly milky as you sift the rice in and out of your fingers. (If you wish to wash the rice, change the water once or twice during the process. Some say washing rice robs it of B-vitamins, however.) Let the rice sit in the bowl for 30 minutes to allow it to absorb some of the water.

Put the rice and the water in the rice cooker and switch it on. After about 25 minutes (depending on the brand of rice cooker), the light will come on, signaling the rice is cooked, and the heat will automatically turn off. Allow the rice to steam for a few more minutes. Place into serving bowls using a wooden spatula.

• It's a bit tricky to get perfect rice using an ordinary pot, but in Japan today, millions of chefs and homemakers still wouldn't dream of using modern technology.

2 cups Japanese rice
2½ cups cold water

Rinse the rice in the water in a large bowl, using your hand as a sieve. Let the rice soak in the water for 30 minutes.

Place the rice and soaking water in a pot and bring to a rapid boil over high heat. Boil for 30 to 45 seconds, then reduce the heat to low, cover tightly, and allow the rice to simmer for 12 to 15 minutes. (Do not lift the cover off during the cooking process, as this will allow steam to escape and affect the fluffiness of the rice.) Remove the pot from the heat and allow the rice to sit and steam another 10 to 15 minutes.

Take off the lid and place into serving bowls using a wooden spatula.

NOTE: If the rice is consistently overcooked or undercooked, adjust the cooking time on the stove ever so slightly until you get it right. (I might add that a gas stove works better than an electric one, for reasons I am unable to explain.)

• This great springtime dish—a simple combination of rice, peas, and spring onions—is surprisingly delicious and satisfying. The textural contrast between the short-grained Japanese rice and the outwardly crisp, inwardly mushy peas provides a little variety in every clump. Often for fun, I break a few *senbei* (rice crackers) into the rice, just to shock a guest. A Japanese would never do such a thing, but the added touch of salt and crunch livens up the dish even further. This recipe yields just enough for an intimate late night supper for two. A Japanese would probably omit the salt, but I think the dish needs some.

Mame Gohan

•

Steamed Rice and Peas

Serves 2

2 cups Japanese rice
1 1/4 cups water
1 tablespoon sake
1/2 cup shelled fresh green peas, parboiled
    (frozen peas will do, if you must)
4 spring onions, quartered

Prepare the rice following the rice cooking method of your choice (see pages 27, 28). Stir in the sake and salt immediately after uncovering the rice. Gently stir in the peas and the spring onions with a wooden spoon, turning the rice over several times to let off steam and to mix thoroughly.

Cover and let sit for 5 minutes to soften the peas and to allow the rice to absorb the oniony perfumes. Serve with miso soup and ice-cold dry Japanese beer.

Kamameshi

•

Japanese Rice Casserole

Serves 2

• Nothing pleases me more in winter than to dig into a hot, steaming *donabe* (earthenware pot) filled with *kamameshi* (one-pot rice casserole). I ate my first one—a nonvegetarian version—at Torigin, an institution famous for *yakitori* (grilled chicken) in the Ginza, the flashiest commercial street in Tokyo.

Kamameshi poses a great challenge for the serious cook. When done exactly right, the rice sticks to the insides of the *donabe*, forming a crackling crust and adding extra texture to the dish. Cooking winter mushrooms and bamboo shoots in with the rice, as in this recipe, gives *kamameshi* a rich, nutlike flavor. Serving this dish alongside spinach in peanut sauce makes a majestic combination.

In Japan during the seventies, this dish was sold in train stations, to be eaten on long train trips. I made the mistake of eating a *kamameshi*, hot in its casserole, while standing up inside the station as I was too hungry to wait for the train to arrive. I was upbraided sternly by the night porter, who informed me that I was being impolite and making a spectacle of myself. When I replied *sumimasen, o-gyogi ga warui* ("excuse me, for my bad behavior"), the man was visibly shaken. "I didn't realize you understood Japanese," he said, "or I wouldn't have meddled in your affairs."

2 cups Japanese rice
1 ounce dried shiitake mushrooms, soaked in water
    for 30 minutes and thinly sliced
1 fresh bamboo shoot, cut into small rectangular pieces
1 ounce *gobo* (burdock root), parboiled
3 1/2 tablespoons sake
2 teaspoons whole-bean soy sauce
Pinch of salt
2 cups *dashi*
1 *negi* (Japanese scallion), finely cut

Rinse the rice in cold water, then drain in a colander and let sit for about 1 hour.

Combine the shiitake mushrooms, bamboo shoots, and *gobo* in a small bowl, and douse with the sake, soy sauce, and salt. Place the rice in a pot and stir in the shiitake mixture, preferably with a wooden spoon. Pour in the *dashi* and cover.

Bring the rice to a boil over medium heat. Reduce the heat to simmer and cook until the casserole is firm on top. Remove the cover and sprinkle the *negi* on top. Cover and let stand for 30 minutes.

If you like a nice crust on the rice, cook over high heat for an additional 2 minutes after the casserole has been allowed to stand.

Japanese
Bibimbab

●

One Bowl
Meal of
Rice and
Vegetables

Serves 2

● I ate *bibimbab* at least once a week when I lived in Tokyo; it is, in fact, my favorite lunch dish in all of Asia.

This dish isn't actually Japanese, but Korean. Served in a large round bowl, *bibimbab* is basically a huge mound of rice topped with different kinds of marinated vegetables, each in its own section, with a fried egg on top and a smear of bean paste on the bowl's rim. The Koreans generally eat the dish with perhaps a dozen strips of seasoned sliced beef between two vegetables. The idea is to mix up the rice, vegetables, and spicy bean paste before you dig in. The amount of bean paste used determines how spicy the dish will be. The Japanese version is relatively mild. In Korea, the dish can make you breathe fire.

$^1/_4$ cucumber, thinly sliced
1 carrot, coarsely chopped
3 dried shiitake mushrooms, soaked in water
        for 30 minutes and thinly sliced
$^1/_3$ cup bean sprouts
2 ounces bamboo shoots, minced
1 tablespoon sugar
Pinch of salt
$^1/_4$ cup sesame oil
1 teaspoon minced garlic
1 tablespoon white sesame seeds
1 egg
1 large leaf romaine lettuce
$1^1/_2$ cups cooked Japanese rice
2 tablespoons *toobanjam* (spicy bean paste),
        or to taste
1 sheet *nori,* sliced into long strips

Sprinkle a touch of salt over the cucumbers, carrots, shiitake mushrooms, and bean sprouts. Let sit for 5 minutes, then pat out the excess moisture with paper towels. (You do not need to do this with the bamboo shoots.) Place each vegetable in a separate bowl.

Combine the sugar, salt, sesame oil, garlic, and sesame seeds. Pour equal amounts of the sesame mixture over each vegetable. Stir-fry the vegetables quickly, one by one, in a cast-iron skillet, starting with the cucumbers, then the bamboo shoots, carrot, shiitake mushrooms, and last, the bean sprouts. (Do not overcook the vegetables; their colors should remain bright.)

Fry the egg sunny-side up in the same pan, making sure that the yolk does not break.

Place the romaine leaf in a large serving bowl, and place the rice on top. Arrange the vegetables on top of the rice in separate sections like slices on a pizza.

Put the egg in the center and a smear of the bean paste along the side of the bowl. Sprinkle with the *nori* and serve.

*Taki Komi
Gohan*

•

*Country-Style
Rice*

Serves 4

• This simple dish makes good use of the rice cooker. An important ingredient here is *sansai* vegetables, which are soaked and salted, and sold in plastic pouches. A dried version is available but is not as flavorful. Because they are unique to Japanese cuisine, *sansai* are available in most Japanese markets, but unfortunately not in other Asian markets.

Sansai translates literally as "wild mountain" and refers to vegetables, roots, and shrubs that grow in the wild—sort of Ewell Gibbons fare, Japanese-style. A typical mix includes *kinnoko* mushrooms, finely chopped sweet potato stems, burdock root, and dropwort, but the mix will vary according to the producer.

3 cups Japanese rice
5 dried shiitake mushrooms
1/2 sheet *abura-age* (deep-fried tofu)
3 tablespoons whole-bean soy sauce
2 tablespoons mirin
1/3 teaspoon salt
3 cups *dashi*
4 ounces brine-packed *sansai* vegetables

Wash the rice 30 minutes prior to cooking and drain in a strainer. Meanwhile, soak the shiitake mushrooms in cold water for 30 minutes. Remove the stems and slice the caps into thin strips. Set aside.

Pour boiling water over the *abura-age* in order to remove excess oil. Drain and slice it into thin strips. Set aside. Combine the soy sauce, mirin, salt, and *dashi* in a large bowl and set aside.

Strain the *sansai* vegetables, then mix them with the shiitake mushrooms and *abura-age*. Fold this mixture into the rice. Place the rice mixture in the rice cooker and pour in the *dashi* mixture.

Steam until the rice is tender and fluffy, according to the rice cooker instructions. Serve immediately.

• This makes a nice replacement for soup on a cold day. Garnish with puréed raw daikon, a smidgen of fresh ginger, lemon juice, and soy sauce.

1 cup Japanese rice
4 cups water
2 to 3 rounded tablespoons white miso, or to taste
5 to 6 ounces silken tofu, broken into little chunks
1 cup fresh spinach, cut into 1/4-inch lengths
1 cup fresh napa cabbage, cut into 1/4-inch lengths
1 to 2 large *umeboshi* (salted, pickled apricot),
    seeded and cut into small pieces
1/8 teaspoon sake or mirin (optional)

Rinse the rice in the water in a large bowl for a minute or two, using your hands as a sieve. Transfer the rice and water to a pot and bring to a boil over high heat. Add the miso and stir to make sure it completely dissolves. (Add more miso or water at this point for desired taste.) Add the tofu, spinach, cabbage, *umeboshi,* and sake.

Bring the mixture back to a boil, cover, and reduce the heat to low. Simmer for 30 minutes, stirring occasionally. Cook longer if you like a more creamy porridge.

Okayu

•

*Home-Style
Porridge*

Serves 3 to 4

Aemono and Sunomono—Mixed Foods and Vinegared Salads

*Isogaba
maware*

*Take the long
way when
you're in a
rush*

*T*HE JAPANESE HAVE an odd relationship with salad, which in the complicated nomenclature of their cuisine can fall under the category of *aemono* (mixed foods), or *sunomono* (vinegared foods). They eat salad for breakfast, for example, with their eggs, *tosto* (thick, sliced toasted bread), and morning coffee. They smother their Western-style salads with creamy French or Thousand Island dressing. And they'll put sugary vegetables, various seaweeds, mushy potatoes, and anything else deemed appropriate in the salad bowl, providing it paints a pretty picture for the eye.

AEMONO

Aemono are the lost children of Japanese cooking, comprising most anything the cook wants to throw together. That leaves room for creativity, but generally, vegetarian *aemono* might mix tofu, eggs, vegetables, seaweeds, roots, and mushrooms in free-form varieties. Nonvegetarian *aemono* are often wildly inventive.

• Iron-rich spinach is one of the most common vegetables on the Japanese table. Unlike Westerners, the Japanese like to eat it cold. The secret to cooking delicious spinach is to wash and drain it well, removing as much grit as possible, and squeezing out any excess moisture. My mother-in-law typically presses the spinach together before serving, leaving it in a dense little green clump. Adding the sesame seeds at the last minute gives this dish a nice contrast in texture.

I (6 ounce) bunch fresh spinach
I teaspoon whole-bean soy sauce
$^{1}/_{2}$ cup *dashi*
I teaspoon sake
I $^{1}/_{2}$ tablespoons white sesame seeds

Fill a large pot with water and bring to a boil. Meanwhile, rinse the spinach carefully, keeping it together in a bunch. Dip the stems in the boiling water for about 10 seconds before letting the entire bunch slide down into the pot. Remove from heat as soon as the leaves are tender, and rinse the leaves under cold running water. Gently squeeze out as much moisture as possible from the spinach, then pat dry with a cloth towel, and place in a bowl.

Combine the soy sauce, *dashi,* and sake in a small pan. Pour the soy sauce mixture over the spinach. Squeeze out the liquid into a separate bowl and pour over the spinach again. Repeat this process two or three more times, ending with the spinach squeezed dry. Press the spinach together into a clump and cut it crosswise into four 2-inch bundles, discarding the bottoms of the stems. Sprinkle with the sesame seeds and serve.

Horenso
Goma Ae

•

Spinach with Sesame

Serves 2

Nira Miso
Goma Ae

•

Garlic Chives
in Miso
Dressing

Serves 2 to 3

• The Japanese prize vegetables such as *nira* (garlic chives), *umeboshi* (salted, pickled apricots), bitter melon, winter melon, and chives, which they claim help the body's acid-base balance. Claims have been made for the cholesterol-lowering effects of garlic, while *umeboshi* are said to cleanse the blood.

Nira are hard to find in Western markets, although most Asian markets stock them. (I usually buy mine in Vietnamese markets.) They cook quickly and have a sharp, pungent flavor. Regular chives may be substituted for them, however, with delicious results. This recipe, a simple *aemono* preparation, is wonderfully satisfying as a side dish or hors d'oeuvre.

1 bundle *nira* (garlic chives) or chives
1 tablespoon corn oil
1 tablespoon miso
2 teaspoons sugar
2 teaspoons sake
1 egg, beaten
1 tablespoon white sesame seeds

Boil the *nira* until they soften, making sure that they do not wilt entirely, about 2 to 3 minutes. Remove from the boiling water, drain, and cut off the white stems. Keeping the *nira* together in a bundle, squeeze out the excess moisture and cut them into slices, 1 to 1 1/2 inches thick. Set aside.

Heat the corn oil in a saucepan over medium heat, and slowly stir in the miso. When the mixture is smooth, add the sugar and sake, stirring gently. Remove the pan from the heat and gradually add the egg, so that it does not coddle. Place the pan over low heat and add the *nira* and sesame seeds, stirring continuously until the egg coddles into tiny pieces. Place clumps of *nira miso goma ae* in round earthenware dishes and serve warm.

● One of the very best *aemono* I ever tasted is this simple combination of sweet, pungent, and acidic elements. Nothing absorbs the flavor of miso like chopped shallots, and they do so with surprising quickness.

3/4 cup white or yellow miso
1 tablespoon mirin
4 ounces shallots, peeled and chopped
Sprinkling of powdered or freshly chopped ginger

Combine the miso with the mirin, and stir in the shallots and ginger. Refrigerate for approximately 2 hours before serving.

Kikuna

Shiro Ae

•

Chrysanthe-
mum Leaf
and White
Miso Dip

Serves 2

• This recipe may be hard to reproduce due to the unavailability of two important ingredients: *kikuna* and *saikyo miso*. *Kikuna* are yellow-green chrysanthemum leaves with a complex, bittersweet flavor. The chrysanthemum is the
flower that represents the Japanese imperial family and as such is of major sig-
nificance both in the hearts and minds of most Japanese. To make a good *shiro-
ae,* it is also helpful to procure the rarest of misos, the prized *saikyo miso,* a
white miso flavored with sake made in the ancient capital of Kyoto. Many upscale Japanese chefs in the U.S. have it sent directly to them from Japan. *Saikyo
miso* and *kikuna* sometimes can be found in the better Japanese markets.

1 teaspoon *saikyo miso*
1 teaspoon mirin
2 tablespoons white sesame seeds
1 tablespoon sugar
1 teaspoon whole-bean soy sauce
1 (6 ounce) bunch *kikuna*
1/2 package firm tofu (about 9 ounces)

Fill a large pot with water and bring to a boil. Meanwhile, combine the miso,
mirin, white sesame seeds, sugar, and soy sauce in a large bowl and set aside.

Place the *kikuna* in the boiling water for 1 minute, then remove from the pot.
Drain the *kikuna* and plunge them into a bowl of ice water and let soak for up
to 5 minutes. Drain and squeeze out the excess moisture. Cut the *kikuna* crosswise into 1-inch lengths.

Grate the tofu using a *suribachi*. You can let it grate on low speed in a
blender, but this will result in a smoother, less traditional, texture. Gently stir
the miso mixture into the tofu, until smooth. Stir in the *kikuna,* one handful at
a time, until the mixture resembles a dense dip. Serve immediately.

• This recipe makes a filling *aemono* that is particularly satisfying on a cold, blustery day. Potatoes and miso go well together and make for a very nutritious snack or light lunch.

4 large russet potatoes
4 to 5 tablespoons red miso
2 cups *dashi*
1 ounce snow peas, stems and strings removed
Pinch of salt

Peel the potatoes and cut each one into 6 pieces. Boil them in lightly salted water for 15 minutes, then drain.

Soften the miso in $^1/_2$ cup of the *dashi,* stirring to dissolve. Using a food sieve, strain out any large chunks of miso remaining. Place the potatoes in the remaining 1 $^1/_2$ cups *dashi* and bring to a boil. Reduce the heat to low, add the miso mixture, and simmer slowly about 15 minutes, until the potatoes are tender but not falling apart. Gently turn the potatoes over every so often to color them evenly.

While the potatoes are cooking, drop the snow peas into rapidly boiling, lightly salted water. Cook the peas about 45 seconds. Plunge them into a bowl filled with ice water to stop the cooking and keep their color bright. Cut them in half lengthwise.

Using a slotted spoon, transfer the potatoes to shallow bowls, pouring a little of the cooking liquid over them. Garnish with the snow peas, points facing up.

SUNOMONO

Sunomono are an essential part of most Japanese meals—breakfast, lunch, and dinner. The term, which translates literally to "marinated things," is one the Japanese use to encompass what we in the West know as salads, as well as other palate-cleansing first courses. *Sunomono* can be anything from shredded cabbage with Thousand Island dressing, a standard inclusion with a set Western breakfast, to vinegared seaweed. It is intended as a refresher, and *sunomono's* persistent lightness makes this course welcome in almost any context.

Goma (sesame seeds) often are sprinkled liberally on marinated dishes. Sesame seeds are by no means native to Japan but were brought into the country fifteen hundred years ago by Chinese or Korean traders. Three colors of *goma* commonly are used: white, the mildest; black, which is rich in calcium; and yellow, the most fragrant. The Japanese say that sesame seeds keep the skin white and the hair black. I enjoy testing the theory.

• *Kyuuri* (cucumber) is a great favorite with the Japanese both as a garnish and as a palate cleanser. The vegetable grows in abundance throughout Japan's cold northern clime, and its crunchy snap adds contrast to more slimy foodstuffs, seaweeds in particular.

This dish is a version of a salad eaten at lunch almost everywhere in Japan. Mrs. Kimiko Jadibi, owner of the Hatsune Ramen House in Van Nuys, California, likes to serve this dish as a teaser alongside one of her gargantuan bowls of ramen. It is disarmingly simple to prepare, yet looks beautiful in a medium-size earthenware or clay bowl. The type of dressing used may be varied. I've included two Japanese dressings to go along with this *sunomono*, though my personal preference is for the first and lighter one.

1 ounce dried *wakame*
1 ounce dried *kombu*
2 gherkin-size cucumbers (see note)
Pinch of salt
2 lemon wedges for garnish
White sesame seeds for garnish

Wash and soak the *wakame* and *kombu* in water in separate bowls for about 30 minutes, or until soft. Peel the cucumbers, and cut them into razor-thin slices. Sprinkle the cucumbers lightly with the salt and allow to sit for no more than 5 minutes. Pat the cucumbers dry with a cloth towel. Place half of the cucumber slices in each of two medium-sized bowls. Place portions of the *wakame* and *kombu* in the bowls in separate sections for maximum visual effect. Garnish each bowl with a lemon wedge.

Pour on *sunomono* or sesame dressing (recipes follow), sprinkle liberally with the sesame seeds, and serve immediately.

NOTE: Japanese cucumbers are best, although they are usually available only during the summer.

• Omit the *aji-no-moto* if you are sensitive to MSG, but I find it boosts the flavor of this dressing.

$^1/_2$ cup rice vinegar
$^1/_8$ teaspoon *aji-no-moto* (optional)
1 tablespoon whole-bean soy sauce
2 tablespoons sugar
$^1/_3$ tablespoon salt
1 tablespoon mirin
1 $^1/_2$ teaspoons sesame oil

In a small pan, combine the vinegar, *aji-no-moto,* soy sauce, sugar, salt, and mirin. Bring to a quick boil over high heat, stirring occasionally. Remove pan from the heat. After the vinegar mixture has cooled, stir in the sesame oil. Chill for 30 minutes.

• This dressing should appeal to those who eat in natural foods restaurants. Apart from crushing the seeds in a Japanese mortar, this recipe is relatively easy and fail-safe. Peanut butter adds a richness that may cause some purists to balk, but I like the flavor, especially with cucumbers.

$^1/_2$ cup white sesame seeds
6 ounces water
$^1/_2$ tablespoon rice vinegar
1 tablespoon whole-bean soy sauce
$^1/_8$ teaspoon salt
$^1/_2$ teaspoon unsweetened peanut butter

Using a *suribachi* or mortar and pestle, crush the sesame seeds until they form a dry paste. Place the remaining ingredients in a blender and blend on low for 2 to 3 minutes while slowly adding the sesame paste. Serve at room temperature.

*Japanese
Green Pepper
and Carrot
Vinegared
Salad*

Serves 2

• Anyone who has been to Japan has noticed the language's odd employment of English; it's mostly charming and funny, but also a bit bizarre. For example, the most famous health drink in Japan is called Pocari Sweat, and I once saw a woman scrubbing the sidewalk wearing a T-shirt that read, "Life's a Bummer."

This simple salad is notable for the contrast between its two main protagonists—one cooked, the other raw. And it's a good palate cleanser, too. If you have trouble finding the smaller, more sharply flavored Japanese green peppers, substitute 2 large green bell peppers.

5 *shishito* (Japanese green peppers)
1 large carrot
1 teaspoon white miso
1 teaspoon sugar
1 1/2 tablespoons rice vinegar
2 tablespoons sesame oil
1 tablespoon white sesame seeds
Pinch of *shichimi* (seven-spice seasoning)

Bring a pot of water to which a pinch of salt has been added to a boil. Cut the green peppers in half, lengthwise, and remove the seeds. Steam the peppers over the boiling water for about 3 minutes. Plunge the peppers into a bowl of ice water, and when they are cold, remove them, and drain. Pat dry with a cloth towel. Slice the peppers into thin spears, and place in a mixing bowl. Wash and peel the carrot. Cut the carrot into rounds and mix with the peppers.

Mix the miso with the sugar. Add the remaining ingredients and mix well. Pour over the vegetables and serve.

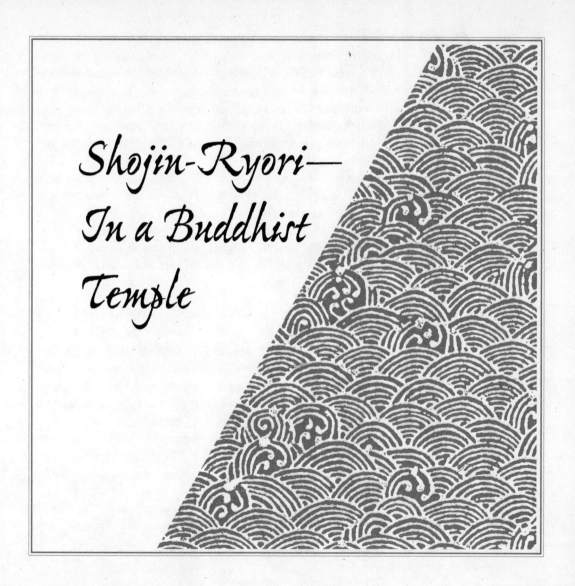

Shojin-Ryori—
In a Buddhist
Temple

*P*ERHAPS THE MOST COMPELLING place to experience Japanese vegetarian cuisine is inside a Buddhist temple, where the highly evolved cuisine known as *shojin-ryori* is served. From ancient times, the cooking philosophy behind *shojin-ryori* has been to offer harmony from the six basic flavors—bitter, sour, sweet, salty, light, and hot. All animal products—including bonito stock—and any vegetables with particularly strong flavors, such as garlic and onions, are shunned because they cause the body to emit strong, animal-like odors.

Buddhist temples are found in every Japanese city, and the majority of Japanese still have Buddhist funerals. Visitors to Japan usually notice that worshipers clap their hands twice after praying, a custom unique to Buddhism. (The worshipers clap to summon up Buddha himself, in the hope that their prayers will be answered.) Kamakura, near Yokohama, and Nara, just outside Kyoto, are both famous for their *daibutsu* (giant gilded statues of Buddha). Koya-san is especially revered because it is said to be the mountaintop from which Buddhism was introduced to Japan, more than one thousand years ago. Today, thirty-two major temples sit atop Koya-san's summit, many of which accept overnight visitors.

According to legend, a young scholar known as Kobodaishi traveled to China in the tenth century, where he schooled himself in Chinese and calligraphy. After two decades, he decided to return to Japan armed with the knowledge of classical Chinese writing and grammar, intending to pass on what he had learned to his countrymen. Along the way, he met—or perhaps envisioned—a hunter accompanied by two enormous dogs. The hunter pointed the way to a forested mountain, where Kobodaishi saw a bright gleam. It was there, he realized, that he would establish his temple, and teach what he had learned to a new generation. Koya-san has been a sacred spot to the Japanese ever since.

To experience *shojin-ryori* myself, I stayed in a temple called Rengejo-in on the holy mountain called Koya-san, located on Japan's rocky Wakayama

Prefecture south of Osaka. You might think that prices in Japan for lodging—and everything else—are exorbitant. But a stay in a Buddhist temple costs less for a room and meals than most hotel accommodations in the U.S. The temple guest rooms are certainly as luxurious as those in a *ryokan* (Japanese hotel), yet cost only a fraction of the price. At a top-level *ryokan* such as Tawaraya or Hiragaya in Kyoto, where millionaires, statesmen, and movie stars stay, the cost sometimes exceeds nine hundred dollars per night. Koya-san's temples have another advantage: They are located away from the neon, electronic sounds, and pollution of modern Japan.

To get to Rengejo-in, I took a long local train ride from Osaka. From there, I entered Wakayama Prefecture, where the train began a steady climb through a dense forest. At the end of the line, I boarded a cable car, which seemed to climb vertically. After reaching the mountaintop, I took a bus to the temple.

When I arrived at the temple gates, I was greeted by one of the head monks, who had been informed of my coming. Other monks were in the kitchen preparing the elaborate vegetarian set courses of dinner and breakfast to be served during my stay.

I then was led through one of the most beautifully tranquil Zen gardens I have ever seen, up a long, narrow staircase skirting the garden's perimeter to a huge guest room. The room had *tatami* (straw mat) floors and was decorated with a flower arrangement, *kakejiku* (scroll paintings), and objets d'art such as a stone bird sculpture. A low, square *kotatsu* (a table with a heating element underneath its top) was the only furniture; it was set for tea and surrounded by colorfully embroidered *zabuton* (cushions). Diners fold their legs under the table, and sit up straight—which is fine, providing their legs do not fall asleep.

One of the young monks then opened the sliding screens, revealing a breathtaking view of the garden, while a second young monk poured green tea into a tiny cup and offered me sweets elegantly wrapped in embossed paper. The young monks then silently excused themselves to allow me to reflect peacefully on the quiet, lovely autumn afternoon. Perhaps as a concession to the modern age, these guest rooms come equipped with televisions. Mine remained off.

About seven that night, I was summoned downstairs to the most attractive room in the temple. The room was filled with art treasures from China, Korea, and Japan: magnificent vases stationed on *tokonoma* (raised places of honor). (A guest in a Japanese home can always tell where he stands in the pecking order. Every formal Japanese room has a *tokonoma,* which resembles a small stage raised from the floor next to one of the room's walls. The closer one sits to the *tokonoma,* the more one is honored. If one is seated next to the exit door, that is not a good sign at all.)

Shortly thereafter, Mrs. Kayumi Soeda, the temple owner and mother of the temple's abbot, came in and introduced herself. Mrs. Soeda is a remarkable woman. She is seventy-five, looks fifty-five, and speaks English as well as most American college students. The Japanese tourist office often sends foreign visitors to Rengejo-in because Mrs. Soeda can explain the food and procedures. Mrs. Soeda enjoys having visitors and practicing her English. But temples are also a business on Koya-san, and guests lend important financial support to the monastic lifestyle.

Mrs. Soeda was the one who told me the story of Kobodaishi in flawless English, occasionally consulting a giant dictionary to verify the more difficult words. She patiently recounted how temples here have lasted through the centuries, constructed of ultra-solid cypress and teak woods in order to withstand the earthquakes that plague the region.

Before retiring, she invited me to join her son and the rest of the monks at six for the entrancing morning prayers. An elaborate dinner was brought in and laid out on the *tatami.* Mrs. Soeda then described each dish and left me to eat in solitude.

The food was dazzling. A small lacquered dish contained an appetizer of *wakame* in a tofu sauce, while a covered lacquered bowl revealed a clear soup fragrant with *yuzu* (Japanese citrus fruit) and laced with slices of Japanese radish. There were *nimono* (simmered dishes), sliced lotus root, steamed pumpkin and *yamaimo* (mountain potato), exquisite tempura of lotus root, *somen* noodles, and *shishito* (Japanese green peppers) no bigger than one's little finger. One covered dish contained a *chawan mushi* (steamed soy-milk custard). As Japanese Buddhists are vegan, they use absolutely no eggs in their cooking.

In the center of the dinner tray was a square of *gomadofu* (a sesame-based food with the consistency of tofu). Around the *gomadofu* were steamed spinach, three kinds of Japanese pickles, a bowl of barley rice, and a few sweets—one a tiny, delicious sugared plum, the other two exquisite grapes, bursting with flavor. The beverage was *matcha* (Japanese green tea) served in a huge ceramic bowl and foamed with a whisk. I ate, and drank, my fill.

Mrs. Soeda peeked in to see that I had finished and to say good night. When I returned to my room, I changed into my *yukata* (bathrobe) and padded downstairs to the temple's scalding cypress bath. The *furo* (bath) purifies the body for sleep. It also makes you feel warm and toasty.

Japanese bath etiquette dictates that you soap off completely before lowering yourself into the water—absolutely no washing in the bath. For the uninitiated, this may be an uncomfortably hot bath, but the experience becomes addictive in short order. When bathing Japanese-style for the first time, be completely still in the water, and the heat will not seem quite so devastating. The first time I had a *furo* in my mother-in-law's home, I jumped in and jumped right back out, my skin the color of a boiled lobster.

After the bath at Rengejo-in, I slept like a baby on a futon the monks had laid out discreetly while I was bathing. At 5:45 A.M., I woke up to the sun peeking over the mountaintop, and I was eager to hear the morning ceremonies.

Walking to the front of the temple on the wooden walkway surrounding the perimeter of the garden, I heard steady chanting. The prayer room loomed in front of me, so I slid back the *shoji* (sliding door screens) and seated myself on the *tatami* reserved for guests. Next to me were two German women, seated *seiza* (legs folded under them). In front of me was an elaborately designed altar, containing a treasure trove of objets d'art from all over Asia framed by gilded wooden beams.

The chanting lasted nearly one hour, after which the abbot, Soeda-san, welcomed us in English; regaled us further of the legend of Kobodaishi, his spiritual master; and invited us to breakfast. The breakfast, simple and delicious, was, in its own way, as aesthetically delightful as the dinner: a bowl of rice gruel, a salted apricot, pickled radishes, a light soup, and a spongy ball of mashed tofu.

It would be nearly impossible to reproduce a *shojin-ryori* dinner in a Western home. The cooks at these temples have been practicing their technique for years, the products are seasonal and many unique to Japan, and the variety of dishes is mind-numbing. I have picked a few recipes typical of this alluring, unusual style of cooking. Eating them, perhaps, will assist the practice of Zen, or in clearing the mind and body.

• *Gomadofu* is my favorite *shojin*-style dish. It is also a staple dish of *sado* (Japanese tea ceremony), which in itself has utensils, rituals, recipes, and etiquette elaborate enough to warrant an entire book. *Gomadofu* is denser and more filling than the usual tofu made from soybeans. Japanese often eat it with a pinch of *wasabi* on top, placed directly in the center. You can prepare the dish the old-fashioned way, using a *suribachi* to grind sesame seeds into a paste, or you can use a food processor. Personally, I'd just go to a Japanese market and buy the ready-made sesame paste.

10 ounces *atari goma* (sesame paste)
9 ounces arrowroot
2 quarts *dashi*
1 cup sake
1 teaspoon salt
3 teaspoons sugar

Combine all the ingredients in a large bowl or pot, mixing well, until the mixture is a smooth paste. Bring the mixture to a light boil over medium heat, stirring constantly with a wooden spatula, then turn down the heat to low. The mixture should be gooey and stick to the spatula.

On the lowest heat possible, stir the mixture almost continuously for 45 to 50 minutes, with gentle motions of the spatula. To check the progress of the mixture, drop a pinch into a bowl of ice water. It should form a stiff clump. Moisten an 8-inch square pan with a bit of water and pour the mixture into the pan. Cool the pan in a bath of shallow ice water, taking care not to submerge more than a third of the pan. Cover the top with plastic wrap and place the pan in the refrigerator for 12 to 15 hours, until the *gomadofu* is entirely solid.

Cut into small squares and garnish with a pinch of *wasabi*. Serve at room temperature.

Renkon
Daikon
Ae

•

Cold Lotus
Root and
White Radish
Salad

Serves 4

• The crunchy, unique vegetable *renkon* (lotus root) is sacred to Buddhism and a fixture in every restaurant serving *shojin-ryori*. In this country, the vegetable is available both fresh and canned, most often in Chinese markets. The one advantage to canned lotus root is how easily it can be sliced. When the vegetable is so prepared, seven or eight tear-shaped holes can be seen in each slice, giving it an artful appearance. Once cooked, lotus rounds provide a good contrast to cubes of crisp raw daikon radish, which makes a refreshing side dish for a formal vegetarian meal.

1 fresh lotus root (6 to 8 ounces)
1 daikon radish (8 to 10 ounces)
1 tablespoon rice vinegar
2 tablespoons whole-bean soy sauce
1/4 cup sake
1/4 cup mirin
1 tablespoon sugar
1/4 cup water

Trim and peel the lotus root. Cut it into thin rounds, between 1/4 and 1/2 inch thick. Peel the radish and cut it into 1-inch rounds, halving and then quartering the rounds until the radish is cubed.

Combine the vinegar, soy sauce, sake, mirin, sugar, and water in a saucepan and bring it to a light boil over low to medium heat. Add the lotus root and allow it to simmer 12 to 15 minutes, until the lotus root softens. Remove the pan from the heat, and allow the lotus root to steep 10 to 15 minutes in the cooking liquid.

Arrange the lotus root on ceramic dishes, with the cubes of raw daikon placed around them. Pour the cooking liquid over the vegetables and serve.

*Kinpira
Gobo*

•

*Simmered
Burdock
Root*

Serves 3 to 4

• Japanese monks live largely off the bounty of the land, so they generally eat a wild diet even a Ewell Gibbons type would envy. *Gobo* is a common Japanese word, but few in the West are familiar with its English equivalent, burdock root. Even peeled and simmered, this fibrous, crunchy stalk is an acquired taste with a curious texture. Modern Japanese prize the burdock root, ascribing to it healing properties that stimulate circulation and help prevent colon cancer.

This is a dish you might find in any Buddhist temple, but it is also one that could turn up on the most Westernized Japanese table. Eat it as a snack or as a colorful side dish.

1 carrot
8 ounces *gobo* (burdock root)
1 tablespoon corn oil
1/2 tablespoon sesame oil
1 tablespoon mirin
1 tablespoon water
2 tablespoons whole-bean soy sauce

Peel the carrot and the burdock root with a vegetable peeler. Cut both into long, thin spears, rinse in ice water, and set aside in separate bowls of ice water to further crisp them.

Combine the corn oil with the sesame oil and heat in an iron skillet, until the pan sizzles slightly. Drain the burdock root and sauté over low heat for 12 to 15 minutes, until it softens slightly. Add the carrot and sauté for 3 to 5 minutes, until tender. Add the mirin, water, and soy sauce, stirring gently. Bring to a fast boil over high heat, then reduce heat and cover. Simmer until all the liquid is gone, about 3 to 5 minutes. Let cool and serve at room temperature.

Poteito

Kuri

Kinton

•

*Mashed
Finnish
Potatoes with
Sweet
Chestnuts*

Serves 4 to 6

• Temple foods tend to be sweet and rich, which brings us to that Japanese standby, the chestnut. A favorite in Japan at dessert time, chestnuts are eaten throughout my favorite season, the one I recently passed on Koya-san—autumn.

Roasted chestnuts are sold in tiny paper bags all over Japan, just as they are in many places in Europe and in some U.S. East Coast cities. In this recipe I've taken the liberty of doing something no Japanese monk would do, and have replaced the yam-like mountain potatoes of the Japanese countryside with delicious yellow Finnish potatoes.

If you use fresh chestnuts, you'll have to go to all the trouble of boiling and peeling them. It's actually better to use jarred chestnuts, available at any upscale food store. You can even halve the sugar and try the recipe with *marrons glacées* from France, horrifically expensive, but sumptuously delicious.

1 pound yellow Finnish potatoes
3/4 cup sugar
pinch of salt
1 ounce mirin
8 ounces chestnuts, preferably in a light syrup

Peel the potatoes and cook in a pan of boiling water, 10 minutes or until tender. Take care not to overcook them; small Finnish potatoes boil to tenderness in less than 10 minutes.

In a large *nabe* (cooking pot), mash the potatoes thoroughly. Slowly add the sugar and the salt. Stir in the mirin, and then add the chestnuts. Simmer the mixture until heated through and let cool.

Spoon into bowls, with about two chestnuts per serving, and serve.

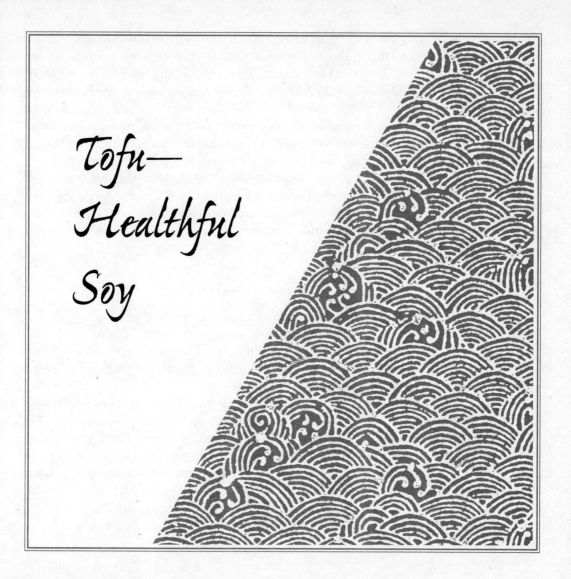

Tofu—
Healthful
Soy

Sannin
yoneba
manju no
chie

Three people
together
have the
wisdom of
Buddha

So much has been written about tofu, a healthful curd made from coagulated soybean milk, that a single chapter seems woefully inadequate. If rice is the heart of Japanese cooking, soybeans—and their many by-products—are the soul. Certain restaurants serve an entire menu of tofu dishes—and nothing else.

Tofu has gained a reputation as a wonder food. A recent report published in many of the major national newspapers proclaimed that eating tofu and other soybean products significantly reduces cholesterol levels. The report first appeared in the July 1995 *New England Journal of Medicine* and was conducted by a University of Kentucky research team. They showed that substituting soybeans for animal proteins in their subjects' diets for six weeks to three months cut total blood cholesterol an average of 9.3 percent. That is good news for lovers of Japanese cuisine.

WHAT IS TOFU?

I had to chuckle when I read a food magazine poll naming tofu as the foodstuff most hated and feared by Americans, beating out worthy opponents such as snails and liver. The fact is, tofu has almost no flavor when eaten by itself, but rather is a foodstuff with the remarkable tendency to absorb the flavor of whatever is cooked along with it.

Legend has it that tofu was invented by a clever Chinese merchant who was forced to repay a debt in meat but ingeniously substituted his creation. The Japanese, historically deprived when it comes to protein, similarly turn to soybeans as a cheap, abundant, and easily cultivated source of the nutrient.

To make tofu, soybeans first are soaked in water overnight and then ground up in a mill. The resulting paste is boiled with some water. A thin skin forms on the surface, which is skimmed off and hung out in sheets to dry. This tofu skin, one of the many by-products of the tofu-making process, is called *yuba*.

The boiling process produces soy milk, a healthful beverage drunk throughout most of East Asia. Strain the milk, and you get a humble pulp the Japanese call *okara* (kind of what whey would be in the dairy world), which is often mixed with vegetables and eaten as an appetizer. Add a coagulant, usually calcium sulfate, to the residue, and the curd, or tofu, is produced.

Many types of tofu are available at a typical Japanese market, often sold water-packed in plastic containers. One of the most popular because it adapts well to cooking is the firm-style *momein-dofu* ("cotton" tofu). *Kinugoshi-dofu* ("silk" or silken tofu) is delicate and custardlike and so is prized by Japanese gourmets. (*Kinugoshi* is also especially good for vegans who wish to make tofu-based desserts such as cheesecake.) One of the better *kinugoshi* tofus is made by Hinoichi and is available at many Asian and Japanese markets.

Another type of tofu, which is used throughout this book, is *abura-age,* or deep-fried tofu. *Gammodoki,* a sort of deep-fried tofu burger made with puréed yams, is available in Japanese markets.

Store tofu in water and refrigerate. Change the water daily to keep the tofu fresh. You can freeze leftover tofu, although freezing changes the texture, making it a bit less firm and more chewy. Defrost the tofu before use, and make sure to squeeze out excess water thoroughly before using.

• *Mapodofu* is essentially a Chinese dish, but it is so popular and ubiquitous in Japanese restaurants around the world that an exclusion would render any chapter on tofu incomplete. This is one of the few truly *karai* (spicy dishes) that Japanese people eat.

Unlike most stewed, simmered, or deep-fried dishes, *mapodofu* is best made in a wok. The first time I tasted the dish in Japan was inside Rei Kyu, a well-known Taiwanese restaurant in the Shibuya section of Tokyo. "Chinese, Japanese, or American?" the waiter asked, so that he could tell the kitchen how much chili paste to add. This version is about as hot as a typical Japanese prefers, but far less hot than any self-respecting denizen of China's Szechuan Province would like.

12 ounces firm tofu
1/5 cup whole-bean soy sauce
2 tablespoons sake
1 tablespoon rice vinegar
1 tablespoon mirin
2 tablespoons Chinese or Vietnamese chili paste,
    available at Asian markets
1 tablespoon grated fresh ginger
1 cup water
1 tablespoon sesame oil
1/5 cup peanut oil
2 cups sliced onion
1 cup sliced fresh shiitake mushrooms or Chinese black mushrooms
2 tablespoons cornstarch dissolved in 2 tablespoons cold water
1/2 cup chopped walnuts

Squeeze the water out of the tofu, cut it into small cubes, and set aside. Combine the soy sauce, sake, vinegar, mirin, chili paste, ginger, and water, and set aside.

Heat the sesame and peanut oils in a wok or frying pan until it begins to sizzle. Stir-fry the onions until light brown. Add the mushrooms and stir constantly, until they are coated in oil and become soft. Pour the soy sauce mixture into the wok and stir-fry for about 1 minute more, then gently spoon in the tofu. Lower the heat and simmer the mixture for about 3 minutes. Add the cornstarch mixture and stir, until the sauce thickens to a glazed, gravylike consistency. Add the walnuts and let simmer for 1 more minute. Serve over Japanese rice.

Agedashi Dofu

•

*Deep-Fried
Tofu*

Serves 2

• The Japanese have dozens, perhaps even hundreds, of different ways in which to eat tofu. One of the easiest and perhaps more indulgent ways is to deep-fry it. This recipe makes a delicious side dish, particularly when one is drinking ice-cold Japanese beer or a flagon of warm sake. The salty, sweet, and high-protein components absorb alcohol, raise the blood sugar, and lift the spirit, all at the same time.

6 ounces silken tofu
1 tablespoon gray salt
4 tablespoons whole-bean soy sauce
2 teaspoons sugar
2 tablespoons finely chopped green onion
1 tablespoon white sesame seeds, ground
4 tablespoons sesame oil
Crumbled *nori* for garnish

Cut the tofu into 2-inch cubes and sprinkle with the gray salt. Make a dipping sauce by mixing the remaining ingredients except for the sesame oil and *nori* in a small glass bowl. Place the dipping sauce on a serving dish.

Heat the sesame oil in a cast-iron skillet over moderate heat until bubbling. Fry the tofu, turning the cubes constantly, until they are golden brown on all sides. Arrange on the serving dish, and garnish with the *nori*.

Summers in Japan are hot and sticky, so the Japanese like to eat foods that, as my wife's family says, "cool you down." *Hiyayakko* is a simple dish, which is served from the most humble sake bar to the most elegant *kaiseki* restaurant. In the summer, no other dish is quite so refreshing or more effective at cleansing the palate. In addition, this is one of the simplest dishes in the Japanese repertoire to prepare, as long as one serves a pleasing dashi or dipping sauce on the side.

1 strip dried *kombu*
1 pound firm tofu, cut into 2-inch cubes
2 tablespoons whole-bean soy sauce
1 sheet *nori*
2 tablespoons grated fresh ginger for garnish
1 green onion, chopped for garnish

Bring 2 quarts water along with the *kombu* to a boil. When the water begins to boil, remove the *kombu*.

Reduce the heat to simmer and add the tofu. Poach the tofu lightly for about 3 minutes. (Make sure that the water level is at least 1 inch higher than the tofu.) Remove the tofu from the pot and plunge the cubes into a bowl of ice water. Allow the tofu to chill thoroughly.

Mix the soy sauce and *nori* in a bowl and set aside. Divide the tofu into three or four portions, and top with the ginger and green onions.

Add a touch of crushed ice to the finished dish if you want the tofu to remain cold. I like to sprinkle *shichimi* (seven-spice seasoning) on my *hiyayakko,* even though my wife's grandmother considers this behavior scandalous.

Hiyayakko

•

*Cold
Garnished
Tofu*

Serves 4

*Tofu
Jambalaya
with
Shimeji-
An*

•

*Tofu
Casserole
with Oyster
Mushroom
Sauce*

Serves 4

• This dish should gladden the hearts of most vegans, though it is probably unrecognizable to traditional Japanese palates. I stumbled across it while undertaking a pilgrimage to natural foods restaurants in Japan, in Osaka's Country Life Restaurant, which is part of an international chain of health food restaurants located in Asia, North America, and Europe. Those who grumble about Japan's high prices can take heart. Many natural foods restaurants in Japan—Country Life, for example—offer all-you-can-eat buffets for about twelve hundred yen, or twelve dollars, for lunch.

The Japanese might consider tofu jambalaya as *okazu* (a side dish), although a vegan would find it suitable as a main course. I find the dish irresistible when paired with a bowl of crunchy *genmai* (brown rice), which most Japanese eat only as a novelty. Feel free to substitute some finely minced garlic for the powdered version. I don't, because I feel that there is enough textural variation in the dish as it is.

THE JAMBALAYA:

1 cup chopped onion
1 cup chopped cooked carrot, wedge cut
1 cup *shimeji* (oyster mushrooms)
1 tablespoon parboiled *hijiki*
1/2 cup shelled fresh green peas (optional)
1/2 tablespoon soybean oil
1 teaspoon onion powder
1/2 teaspoon salt
1/8 teaspoon garlic powder
1 tablespoon plus 2 teaspoons whole-bean soy sauce
12 ounces firm tofu

THE *SHIMEJI-AN:*

1 cup *shimeji* (oyster mushrooms)
1 teaspoon soybean oil
1 cup water
1 tablespoon plus 2 teaspoons whole-bean soy sauce
Pinch of salt
$^1/_4$ cup cornstarch or *katakuikko* (Japanese potato starch)
    dissolved in $^1/_4$ teaspoon water

Preheat the oven to 350 degrees F and lightly oil a baking dish.

To prepare the jambalaya, lightly sauté the onion, carrot, *shimeji, hijiki,* and fresh peas in the soybean oil in a large frying pan. When the onions begin to take on a light golden sheen, remove the pan from the heat. In a large bowl, combine the onion powder, salt, garlic powder, and soy sauce. Slowly crumble in the tofu, so that it resembles hard scrambled eggs. Slowly fold in the sautéed vegetables, and place the jambalaya in the baking dish. Bake for 20 minutes.

Meanwhile, prepare the *shimeji-an.* In a cast-iron pan, sauté the *shimeji* in the soybean oil, until they brown. Combine the water, soy sauce, and salt in a small bowl, and slowly pour the mixture into the skillet, stirring constantly. Slowly stir in the cornstarch, until the sauce thickens. Pour the sauce over the jambalaya and serve.

NOTE: The jambalaya may be steam-cooked, rather than baked, in a Japanese steamer for the same amount of time, or until it is soft and fluffy.

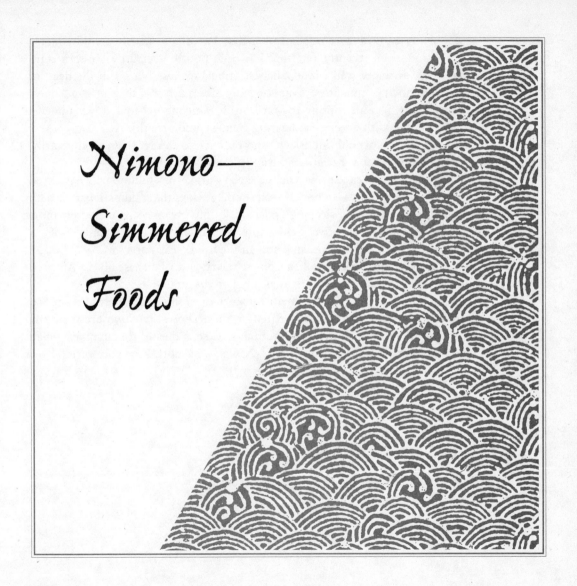

Nimono— Simmered Foods

Tenki wa

nibutsu wo

ataezu

Heaven

bestows but

one talent

*I*T IS IMPORTANT to remember that Japan is primarily a cold country and, until recently, one that has been poorly heated by Western standards. How well I remember entering Japanese houses in the dead of winter, removing my shoes, squeezing my size 12 feet into pint-sized guest slippers, and then attempting to warm up by shoving my folded legs under a *kotatsu* (table with an electric heating element underneath). After only a few minutes, my legs would fall asleep, and I'd have to retract them momentarily, thereby losing whatever heat I had trapped under the table.

The Japanese have their own tricks to keep warm. They traditionally have lived in poorly insulated wooden houses—one of the reasons the scalding Japanese bath evolved, not to mention sleeping under thick down blankets. A clever Japanese joke pokes fun at the native architecture: For a happy life, a Japanese wife, a Chinese cook, an American salary, and an English house. For a miserable life, an American wife, an English cook, a Chinese salary, and a Japanese house. Amen to the last part, at least whenever there is snow on the ground.

This brings us to the gargantuan category of *nimono*, the stewed dishes so common in Japan, and so rarely eaten on these shores. *Nimono* are the heart and soul of most Japanese home dinners, except during the summer, when lighter, less warming fare is consumed. *Nimono*, in short, keep you warm.

• I hereby confess an emotional attachment to *oden,* even though to non-Japanese, it tends to be one of the more bizarre and inaccessible dishes the cuisine has to offer. *Oden* is best described as simmered vegetables in hot broth, but the vegetables are typically cut into large, oddly shaped pieces that often are as strange to the eye as to the palate.

When I first lived in Japan during a particularly cold winter, I occupied a four-and-one-half-*tatami* (straw mat) room known as a *yojoohan*—normal for young Japanese men, perhaps, but fairly absurd for a two-hundred-plus-pound Westerner such as myself. The room was cold—and so almost nightly, after eleven and my ritual visit to the *sento* (public bathhouse)—I would amble over to the nearest *yatai* (covered portable food stall), and partake of *oden.*

It was not a vegetarian *oden,* but one that included *kamaboko,* the fish paste cakes of various shapes and colors—pink, green, and orange. Almost all of the *kamaboko* taste the same, which is to say tasteless to all but the most evolved palates, so nothing is lost in my omitting them from this recipe.

The seriousness of the *oden* meal is evident in its preparation. In Osaka, there is a famous *oden* restaurant called Tako-Ume ("the octopus and the plum" would be a colorful translation). There, the water in the restaurant's enormous wooden kettle constantly steams off boiling stock that is replaced by wooden buckets filled with fresh water. At night, when the restaurant closes, the flame is turned down as low as it will go, but never off, so that the contents cook continuously. No one has emptied, or cleaned, the kettle since 1897, the year Tako-Ume opened.

My version takes considerably less time to prepare.

Oden

•

*Simmered
Vegetables
in Broth*

*Serves 3 as
a main dish,
4 to 5 as a
snack*

- $^1/_2$ pound tofu, preferably silken
- $^1/_8$ cup flour
- 1 tablespoon corn oil
- 6 ounces daikon radish
- 6 ounces *konnyaku* (jellied yam cake
  sometimes called "devil's tongue")
- 4 ounces *abura-age* (deep-fried tofu),
  cut into $1^1/_2$-inch squares
- 4 hard-boiled eggs
- $1^1/_2$ to 2 quarts *dashi*
- 2 tablespoons whole-bean soy sauce
- 1 tablespoon mirin
- 1 teaspoon salt
- 1 carrot, cut into $^1/_2$-inch rounds
- 1 cup julienned *hakusai* (napa cabbage)
- 2 *yamaimo* (Japanese mountain yams), julienned
- 1 large, or 2 small potatoes, julienned

Rinse the tofu in cold water, and pat dry with a cloth towel. Place tofu on a dish in the refrigerator for 15 minutes. Drain off the water at the bottom of the dish, and cut the tofu into cubes. Dredge the tofu cubes lightly in the flour. In a cast-iron skillet, fry the tofu in the corn oil until slightly browned. Remove the tofu from the skillet and drain on paper towels.

Peel the radish, and cut it into rounds. Cut the *konnyaku* into 2-inch equilateral triangles. You now have round, square, and triangular shapes for the stew pot.

Heat up the *abura-age* in a cast-iron skillet without oil, and when it becomes hot and sizzling, remove from the pan and drain on paper towels.

In a large *nabe* (cooking pot), combine the *dashi,* soy sauce, mirin, and salt, and bring to a boil over high heat. Add the daikon, carrot, and *hakusai,* and cook for 12 to 15 minutes, or until vegetables are tender. Add the *yamaimo* and potatoes, and reduce heat to a simmer. Cook on the lowest heat possible for about 30 to 40 minutes.

If you like a sweeter *oden,* add a bit of sugar before simmering. It could be psychological, but I'd swear the *oden* comes out better when the pot is covered by a wooden cover called an *otoshi-buta,* which has a wooden slat running down the center. Japanese traditionally eat this dish with *karashi,* a powdered mustard mixed with water into a paste that's hot enough to bring tears to the eyes.

Takenoko

Nimono

•

*Simmered
Young
Bamboo
Shoot*

Serves 3 to 4

• This dish is typically found in *bento,* the Japanese lunch box assemblage of cold and cooked dishes served in compartmentalized lacquered boxes. Good *bento* ranks among the very best of meals available in natural foods restaurants throughout Japan. Many components in *bento* are simmered or stewed, and *nimono* are considered healthful by the Japanese. In the city of Kanazawa on the Japan Sea, *go dan bento* (five drawers lunch box) is one famous specialty—a mix of local seafoods and vegetables, with each drawer representing a different course in the Japanese lunch.

A memorable natural foods *bento* lunch is served at a Tokyo restaurant called Healthy-kan, just three minutes from the J R Ichigaya Station. The chef there presented a lunch box alongside a simple bowl of soup with egg and *kombu.* The box contained a bottom drawer of Japanese pickles and brown rice, and a top drawer of goodies, including sweet pumpkin, cooked carrot, sautéed *hijiki,* steamed spinach, sesame tofu, simmered black beans, apple in cream sauce, an interesting side dish called *kinnoko natto kombu* (a glutinous dish of mushrooms stewed with shredded kelp), and *takenoko* (young bamboo).

Take is the generic Japanese word for bamboo, but the *no-ko* suffix, which means "child of," is added to refer to the part of the vegetable that Japanese people eat, namely the tenderest inner leaves. This rustic winter vegetable is simple to prepare—one reason it is a main component of *o-setchi-ryori,* the foods Japanese people eat to celebrate their New Year break.

The Japanese New Year, which starts the same day as our own, lasts four to five days, during which time homemakers get a break. It is the only time during the year when they do not cook, as the simmered dishes are made in advance and have a long life after cooking. An added advantage of *takenoko* is their ability to absorb oil—nearly thirty times their weight—in the stomach. That is one reason why oily Chinese dishes use them so liberally.

1 quart *dashi*
1 tablespoon whole-bean soy sauce
2 tablespoons mirin
1 teaspoon rice vinegar

Combine the *dashi,* soy sauce, mirin, and vinegar in a *nabe* (cooking pot) and bring to a slow boil over low heat, adding the bamboo when the liquid starts to boil. Reduce the heat and simmer for 30 to 40 minutes, until the bamboo shoots are tender.

Takenoko are delicious hot, but they also can be served cool, placed in a *bento* along with your favorite dishes. For a more natural taste, water may be substituted for the *dashi.*

• Autumn is my favorite season in Japan. The weather typically is gorgeous throughout Honshu and Kyushu during October, while November brings some of the most spectacular foliage anywhere in the world. As in the West, autumn also brings the pumpkin harvest. Japanese love pumpkin, whether eating it at an Anna Miller's pie shop inside a crust or in this form, one of the most common *nimono* throughout Japan.

Most Japanese recipes call for brown sugar when cooking pumpkin, but I'm a native New Englander, which makes me especially fond of both autumn colors and maple sugar. Serve the pumpkin as a side dish in a *bento,* or eat it steaming hot with rice and a green vegetable.

$1^{1}/_{2}$ pounds pumpkin
4 cups *dashi*
1 tablespoon whole-bean soy sauce
2 tablespoons pure maple syrup
1 tablespoon mirin
2 tablespoons sake

Remove the hard outer layer from the pumpkin and quarter it. Scrape out the seeds and cut the pumpkin into large $1^{1}/_{2}$-inch chunks.

In a *nabe* (cooking pot) or a cast-iron skillet, combine the *dashi,* soy sauce, maple syrup, mirin, and sake, and bring to a boil over medium heat. Stir in the pumpkin, reduce the heat, cover, and simmer for 10 to 15 minutes, or until tender and the syrup forms a light glaze. If you have an *otoshi-buta* (wooden cover), place the lid directly on the pumpkin while it is simmering.

• Autumn is also the time Japanese people hear booming voices emanating from mobile loudspeakers. During my first November in Japan, I thought the voices were auguring some sort of political movement, like the Bolshevik Revolution.

My imagination got the best of me. The voices, crying out *yamaimo* and *satsumaimo,* it turned out, were those of pushcart sellers who were hawking different kinds of hot potatoes—masterpieces wrapped in foil and ready to fill a hole in the stomach. Americans are used to the jingling bells on an ice-cream truck. In Japan, it is "get your potatoes while they're hot."

The Japanese revere all members of the potato family, not just their small sugary ones, their mealy mountain yams, and their large yellow potatoes. This recipe calls for new potatoes and sweet basil. Japanese basil is *shiso,* really the beefsteak plant in English, and its pungent, perfumy essences are used in pickling and added to fried dishes. For new potatoes, though, *aoshiso,* their word for our green basil, works better.

1 1/2 pounds new potatoes, skins left on
2 tablespoons corn oil
2 quarts dashi, or enough to completely cover the potatoes
2 tablespoons red miso
2 tablespoons mirin
3 small bunches sweet basil, minced

Wash the potatoes in cold water and pat them dry. In a cast-iron skillet, sauté the potatoes in the oil for 4 to 5 minutes, until they take on a golden color. Add the *dashi,* miso, and mirin, and bring to a slow boil over low heat, allowing the broth to almost completely evaporate, about 20 minutes. (If the potatoes are still watery, pour off a little of the broth and turn up the heat.) While there is a bit of liquid left, add the basil, stirring and shaking the pot so that the basil mixes in thoroughly. Serve immediately.

Poteito
Aoshiso
Miso
Nimono

•

Simmered New Potato with Sweet Basil and Miso

Serves 3 to 4

Mushimono—
Steamed
Foods

*Zu kan soku
netsu*

*Keep your
feet warm
and your
head cool*

STEAM COOKING IS ONE of the most healthful and natural ways to prepare foods. You don't need a recipe to steam vegetables in a bamboo or metal steamer. Just cut up the vegetables, place them in a steamer over boiling water, and a short while later, prepare to taste. Sprinkle them with soy sauce and *shichimi* and presto—you've got Japanese-style vegetables.

Nearly any Chinese or Asian market sells round bamboo steamers, which have slats on the bottom, wooden sides, and woven bamboo covers. In Chinese cooking, the steamers often are placed directly into a wok. For Japanese dishes, you can place the steamer directly atop two or three inches of water in a pot, making sure that the foods inside do not come into direct contact with the water itself. Most health food stores sell metal contraptions that fan out to fit the shape of the pots in which they are placed. The fan blades are riddled with holes, which allow the steam to penetrate the foods. My Japanese friends claim to be able to tell the difference between foods cooked in metal or bamboo. At any rate, the bamboo steamer certainly looks more Japanese.

The steamed course of a Japanese meal is an important part of the traditional *kaiseki* (multicourse meal). It typically is served between the courses called *suimomo* (clear soups) and *agemono* (fried foods). Occasionally, Japanese steam sweets, too. *Mushi-yookan* is a popular sweet made by mixing together *an* (azuki bean and sugar paste) with wheat flour and boiled chestnuts, then steaming the mixture in a rectangular pan.

• A few of my Japanese friends consider this unusually colorful dish *hade* (flashy). The orange carrot, white tofu, yellow *yuba* and green spinach purée look especially bright in contrast to the earth tones normally found in good Japanese pottery. Chef Koji Yoshida of Shihoya Restaurant in Los Angeles prepares a nonvegetarian version and serves it in a plain glass dish, so as not to mute the colors.

Tofu
Hakata
Mushi

•

Steamed
Tofu with
Winter
Vegetables

Serves 4

2 ounces dried *yuba,* soaked for 30 minutes in cold water
18 to 19 ounces firm tofu
1 large carrot, parboiled
1/4 cup sake
1/4 cup *dashi*
Pinch of salt
1/4 cup Japanese potato starch

Cut the tofu widthwise into 6 slices, then cut each slice lengthwise in half to yield 12 thin slices. (The slices should be no more than 3/4 inch wide.) Remove the *yuba* from the soaking water and drain. Cut the *yuba* into 12 slices to closely resemble the shape of the sliced tofu. Cut the carrot lengthwise into thin slices that will fit nicely atop the tofu and *yuba.*

Remove the stems from the spinach, rinse the leaves, and boil them for 3 minutes. Remove the spinach from the pot and purée it in a blender with the sake, *dashi,* and salt. Set aside.

On a piece of plastic wrap, stack the tofu, *yuba,* then carrot in layers, sandwich-style, sprinkling a little potato starch between each layer. Wrap the stack tightly in the plastic wrap. Steam the stack in a flat bamboo steamer over low heat for 20 minutes. Remove the stack from the steamer, take off the plastic wrap, and cut the stack into cubes. Serve cubes atop the spinach purée.

Steamed
Custard in
Tea Bowls

Serves 5

• Nothing brings out the inner child more than digging into a *chawan* (ceramic bowl) filled with a light egg custard, and fishing out a prize such as a gingko nut, an enoki mushroom, or a nugget of chestnut, hidden at the bottom.

I first ate homemade *chawan mushi* at the home of my in-laws in Yokohama. Though it contained nonvegetarian items such as chicken and fish, it filled my imagination with all sorts of possibilities. The following version is atypical of the ones found in ordinary Japanese homes. Note that the *chawan* are placed directly on the water, as opposed to inside a steamer.

6 dried shiitake mushrooms
1 ounce enoki mushrooms
8 chestnuts, steamed and halved
8 fresh snow pea pods, cut crosswise in half
2 green onions, finely chopped
4 eggs, beaten
1 tablespoon gray salt
1 teaspoon freshly ground pepper
1 tablespoon sake
3 cups *dashi*
10 spinach leaves

Wash and place the shiitake mushrooms in a pot and cover them with water, then bring to a boil. Remove the pot from the heat and let stand for at least 1 hour. Remove the shiitakes from the pot and drain. Combine the shiitakes, enoki, chestnuts, pea pods, and green onions. Place equal portions of the vegetable mixture in the bottom of 5 *chawan*.

Mix together the eggs, salt, pepper, sake, and *dashi*. Pour equal amounts of the egg mixture over the vegetables in the *chawan*. Place 2 spinach leaves on top of each *chawan*, then cover with their ceramic lids. (If you buy *chawan* at a Japanese store, the lids generally are included.)

Place the *chawan* directly into a large cast-iron pan containing about 3 inches of water. Cook over low heat for 15 to 20 minutes, or until custard is firm. Serve with slices of *yuzu* (Japanese citrus fruit), if available.

*Asparagus
Yubamaki*

•

*Asparagus
Yuba Roll*

Serves 4

• The suffix *maki,* when applied to the name of a dish or recipe, always indicates a type of roll, whether a handroll in a sushi bar, a *harumaki* (spring or egg roll), or something you can steam, as in this easy recipe. Since asparagus is seasonal, you won't be able to make this dish year-round. When asparagus isn't available, substitute a mixture of *gobo* (burdock root) and carrot.

2 ounces *yuba,* soaked in cold water for 30 minutes
1/2 pound fresh asparagus
2 tablespoons Japanese potato starch
6 ounces firm tofu
1 ounce dried *wakame*
Pinch of salt
1/2 cup *sumiso* sauce, available in Japanese markets

Drain the *yuba* and lay it out in a large square on top of a piece of plastic wrap. Boil the asparagus over medium heat for 13 to 14 minutes, or until tender. Arrange the asparagus on top of the *yuba,* and sprinkle evenly with the potato starch.

Mash the tofu with the *wakame.* Spread the tofu mixture evenly over the asparagus. Sprinkle with the salt. Starting from one end, roll up the *yuba* into a cylinder, taking care that the asparagus does not protrude from either end. Pinch each end closed and wrap tightly in the plastic wrap. Steam the roll in a bamboo steamer for 20 minutes. Remove the roll from the steamer and take off the plastic wrap. Cut the roll into 4 equal pieces. Top with the *sumiso* sauce and serve.

• This simple dish is adapted from a recipe by Ryo Sato, owner of Chez Sateau, a French restaurant in Arcadia, California, and Daruma, a Japanese pub in Gardena. It actually is more of an *itamemono* (steam-sautéed foods) than *mushimono*. Omit the touch of sesame oil if you find its intense taste too strong for the delicate perfume of the broccoli stems.

Brokkori

Ninjin

Kinpira

•

*Steam-
Sautéed
Broccoli and
Carrot with
Savory
Dressing*

Serves 4

8 ounces broccoli stems
2 ounces carrot
1 1/2 tablespoons peanut oil
1/4 cup light soy sauce
1 tablespoon mirin
2 teaspoons sugar
1 tablespoon sesame oil
Pinch of salt
Pinch of ground red pepper or *shichimi*
    (seven-spice seasoning)
1 teaspoon white sesame seeds

Peel off the hard outside layer of the broccoli stems, making them uniformly cylindrical. Cut the stems so that they are no more than 2 inches long. Peel the carrot, and trim and cut it until the pieces are roughly the same size as the broccoli stems.

In a cast-iron skillet, heat the peanut oil until it sizzles slightly. Add the carrot, then the broccoli, and sauté quickly until tender.

Stir in the soy sauce, mirin, sugar, and sesame oil. Add the salt and red pepper, adjusting the seasoning to taste. Remove the skillet from the heat and let the vegetables steam in the skillet for about 1 minute. Do not overcook; the vegetables should be *al dente*. Transfer vegetables to a serving dish and sprinkle with the sesame seeds. Serve immediately.

Edamame

•

*Steamed
Green Soy
Beans*

Serves 2

• Go to virtually any Japanese pub, or *sakaba,* and a bowl of steamed green soy beans is served as a complimentary appetizer. Nothing tastes better with a cold dry Japanese beer, and I love the way the beans pop out of their pods and into your mouth. There is no trick to cooking them once you find the texture you like best. Just salt the beans lightly and pour a little light soy sauce over them.

6 ounces green soy beans
pinch salt
light soy sauce to taste

Steam the unshelled green soy beans in a bamboo steamer over rapidly boiling water for exactly 8 minutes. Transfer them to 2 bowls and sprinkle with salt, then refrigerate until they are slightly chilled. Serve with the light soy sauce.

Agemono—
Fried
Foods

Yoojin ni
shiru
horobizu

A fortress
cannot be
stormed
casually

EVERYWHERE YOU GO in Japan, you are likely to smell things frying. In my view, what sets Japanese fried foods above those in other cuisines is the country's obsession with freshness. Rarely—if ever—will old, smoky, or discolored oil be used in a respectable home or restaurant. And never is that more true than with the delicacy known as tempura, perhaps the world's most artful frying technique.

• I learned to speak Japanese in a *sakaba* (local pub). All my friends assumed I learned the language from my wife, but that was not the case. Pillow talk may be the best way to learn a new language, but when I met Keiko-san, I knew no Japanese, and so our relationship always has seemed more natural with English.

Pub Japanese is rough, dominated by men's slang and abrupt phraseology. Those who do not speak Japanese are often astonished to discover that men's and women's language can differ not only in pitch, tone, and morphology, but even in syntax. That's one more reason why I never spoke Japanese with my wife. Most of the things I learned in the pub made her blush.

Japanese pub food is terrific, but tends to be salty.—all the better to promote a thirst. Here is a delicious recipe for a simple savory. The mix of sesame oil and soy sauce soaks right into the eggplant, making this a perfect dish to serve with an ice-cold beer and some spicy rice crackers.

4 Japanese eggplants
1 tablespoon sesame oil
2 tablespoons whole-bean soy sauce
1 tablespoon sake

Slice the eggplants crosswise into slices approximately $1/4$ inch thick. In a cast-iron skillet, fry the eggplants in the oil on both sides for 10 minutes over high heat, adding the soy sauce and the sake. When the eggplant is nicely browned, simmer over low heat until the sauce thickens, and serve.

Nasu No Oradani

•

Eggplants Fried in Sesame Oil

Serves 4

• Here in the West, we are more than familiar with the sushi counter. In Japan, several first-class restaurants also have tempura counters, where in my view, one of the most exquisitely satisfying meals in the entire country can be had. Tempura, though, is not native to Japan. Portuguese traders brought the frying method into the country during the sixteenth century, and it has been a noble addition to the Japanese kitchen ever since. The etymology of the word is unclear: Some say it is derived from the Portuguese word for temple. Others have declared it was taken from *tempora*, Portuguese for lent.

On my last visit to Kyoto, I ate in a first-class tempura restaurant, Yoshikawa Inn, also fabled as a *ryokan* (Japanese hotel). A luxurious tempura *kaiseki* (multicourse meal) at the inn starts at one hundred dollars per person. But first-class tempura restaurants also cater to businesspeople with little time to spare, and prices for lunch begin at as little as twenty dollars. This proves to be not only a great bargain, but an incomparable taste treat as well.

When entering a tempura counter such as the one at Yoshikawa Inn, you must first remove your shoes and don slippers. At the inn, you walk across several springy *tatami* (straw mats), which lead up to a series of *noren* (hanging cloth curtains). As in all Japanese restaurants, the greeting *irasshaimase* ("please come in") is uttered. Once inside the tiny room, you are led to a seat at the U-shaped counter, behind which a uniformed chef is standing, awaiting your order. Tea is brought, then *zensai* (appetizers) to wake up the palate.

First, you will be introduced to the chef, who will probably bow with the flourish of an orchestra conductor. Order a tempura course, and the chef will prepare your order piece by piece, selecting each morsel from a beautifully arranged basket of foods. He batters the item, plunges it into hot oil, allows it to cook, then fishes it out with a golden wire basket, and finally places it on your plate with a deft turn. A kimono-clad waitress, meanwhile, has been busy replenishing your tea, bringing you a bowl of rice, a lacquered bowl of hot miso soup, and some *tsukemono* (pickles). A tiny ceramic pitcher of dipping sauce, to be poured into an accompanying dish, is also on the counter. In the postage-stamp-sized dish next to your left hand, you will find freshly ground salt to dip the tempura in. Soy sauce? Banish the thought.

You might start with a humble slice of carrot, or perhaps *shishito* (Japanese green pepper). Later, perhaps, would come eggplant, leek, pumpkin, more luxurious vegetables such as shiitake mushrooms, and even asparagus, if in season. If you are not a vegetarian, you might have something such as *tai* (red snapper) or *ebi* (whole prawns). When the course is finished, you should feel free to order *okawari* (seconds)—though you will be charged à la carte for each piece—which could be anything from *somen* noodles in a tiny clump to chestnuts, sea eel, or fresh scallops.

Perhaps the most remarkable thing about a skilled tempura chef is his ability to juggle orders. He must be able to keep track of every diner—not only what they have eaten but where they are in their courses. He must cook every piece to perfection, a delicate golden brown. Good tempura requires that the batter be light and crunchy, never sodden with grease the way it so often is outside Japan. This takes practice. The batter must not be overmixed; the oil temperature must be precisely 340 degrees F; and the cooking time, which varies slightly from item to item, must be tracked. To paraphrase an anonymous gourmet who was referring to great schnitzel, "One should be able to sit on great tempura without getting a grease stain on the pants." So far, I haven't achieved that kind of perfection.

Bear in mind that the kind of frying oil can vary. In Osaka and Kyoto, for instance, many restaurants—and Yoshikawa Inn is one—use soybean oil. In Tokyo and the Kanto region, many great establishments—the great Inagiku for instance—use a mixture of peanut and sesame oil, similar to the one used in my recipe. (Vegans and natural-food enthusiasts can also experiment with safflower, canola, and other healthful oils that have a relatively high smoking point.)

When preparing the recipe that follows, remember that the batter should not be overmixed; it should be slightly lumpy. Overly smooth batter results in the excess absorption of oil, which is fatal to good-quality tempura. And finally, always make sure the oil is fresh. Renowned restaurants such as Inagiku, it is rumored, bottle and sell their once-used oil to second-class tempura establishments. The stories may be apocryphal, but I think not.

THE BATTER:

Pinch of salt
1 1/2 cups flour
2 egg yolks
1 cup cold water

THE DIPPING SAUCE:

1/4 cup *dashi*
1 tablespoon sake
2 tablespoons mirin
2 tablespoons whole-bean soy sauce
Freshly grated daikon radish (optional)

THE TEMPURA:

1 1/2 cups peanut oil
1/2 cup sesame oil
20 string beans, washed, ends removed, and halved
2 Japanese eggplants, cut into 3-inch strips
1 *renkon* (lotus root), peeled and cut into thin slices
1 carrot, peeled and cut into 1/2-inch strips lengthwise
6 spears asparagus, halved
12 spring onions, outer layer of skin removed
12 *shishito* (Japanese green peppers)
4 ounces pumpkin, cut into bite-sized chunks

To make the batter, sift the salt in with the flour. Beat the egg yolks into the cold water, then slowly and lightly mix this into the flour, making sure a few lumps remain. Set aside.

To make the dipping sauce, mix the *dashi,* sake, mirin, and soy sauce together and warm over low heat in a saucepan. If you prefer, add the daikon to the sauce, though in Japanese restaurants, it is placed in tiny clumps on the individual serving dishes.

To make the tempura, heat the sesame and peanut oils in a deep fryer, wok, or large saucepan to 340 to 350 degrees F. To test for the proper temperature, drop a small ball of batter into the oil. If the ball floats immediately to the surface, the oil is the right temperature.

Dip the vegetables, one by one, into the batter and give them a turn, then transfer them into the oil with a wire basket. As soon as you plunge the vegetables into the hot oil, large bubbles should sizzle around the vegetables. When the bubbles become tiny, like the mousse in expensive champagne, the tempura is done. The batter should be a fine light gold, not a deep golden-brown. (Fry as many pieces of vegetable as you can, although most people are content to fry about a half-dozen pieces at a time.) Drain the tempura momentarily on paper towels.

Transfer the tempura to individual serving dishes and eat immediately, dipping in the dipping sauce or salt, if you prefer. In Japanese restaurants, dipping sauce customarily is served in tiny individual sauce dishes and the diner adds as much grated daikon as desired. Some Japanese like to eat grated fresh *wasabi* (horseradish) with their tempura. I do not.

Natto Gyoza

•

Pot Stickers
with
Fermented
Soybean
Paste

Serves 2 to 3

• *Gyoza* are the delicious fried dumplings that are the perfect accompaniment to a cold glass of beer on a muggy Japanese summer day. Oddly enough, the dish is one of the only provinces of the male in Japanese home cooking, and hence the dumplings have traditionally been stuffed with a minced meat mixture.

This version relies on a *natto* filling instead of the usual minced pork and spices. *Natto* is a fermented soybean paste with an unusually strong odor that foreigners living in Tokyo either love or hate. It is notorious throughout Japan as being a food only people from Tokyo will eat. In my travels, however, I discovered that the Japanese north of Tokyo seem to love *natto,* too, while on the islands of Kyushu and Shikoku, and in the Osaka-Kobe region of Japan, many people regard it as most unappetizing.

Cooking *natto* reduces its fragrance. But a word of caution: saying *natto mo taberareru* ("I can eat *natto*") is taken by Japanese to mean you'll eat anything in their cuisine. That alone should give you an idea that this is no neutral flavor.

3 ounces *natto*
$^{1}/_{4}$ cup finely chopped onions
4 cloves garlic, peeled
Handful of *shiso* (Japanese basil), finely chopped
Dash of soy sauce
2 (4-ounce) packages *gyoza-no-kawa* (gyoza wrappers),
    available at Japanese markets
Sesame oil for sealing wrappers
Corn oil for frying

Mix the *natto,* onions, garlic, *shiso,* and soy sauce together in a bowl. Spoon enough of the *natto* mixture, about 1 tablespoon, onto a *gyoza* wrapper. Moisten the edges of the wrapper with a touch of sesame oil. Fold in half, and pinch the edges to seal. Repeat the process until all the wrappers are used.

Pan-fry the *gyoza* over medium heat in the corn oil for 3 to 4 minutes. When the *gyoza* are light brown on both sides, add an inch of water to the pan to produce steam. Cover the pan and cook for 6 to 7 minutes.

NOTE: Do not use sesame or peanut oil to fry the *gyoza.* Their flavors are too strong for this dish.

• My mother-in-law Hiroko makes terrific *koroke,* a Japan-ized word derived from the French word croquette. Hiroko, like most Japanese, is totally unable to pronounce French.

The Japanese have adapted hundreds of European dishes to their own kitchen, and in the process, have corrupted both the recipe and the pronunciation. *Monburan,* which an American might guess was a breakfast cereal, is really the way the chestnut-loving Japanese pronounce the French dessert classic Mont Blanc, a mound of whipped cream and chestnut purée.

I've added sweet corn to Hiroko-san's recipe, paying homage to an American classic, the sweet corn fritter. It's delicious eaten as a savory alongside a couple of *onigiri,* but it is also a filling main course. Legend says *koroke* are a Japanese creation, made by a chef said to have invented it for the Meiji emperor who looked to the West for some of his inspirations. I think it's more likely that an early-twentieth-century graduate student brought back a recipe after a stint in Paris. All I know is that *koroke* got me in big trouble once.

On my second visit to my wife's family home, I peeked my nose into the kitchen to see what Hiroko-san was frying. When I came out, there was a stony silence. "What did I do wrong?" I asked, noting how displeased my fiancée's father was. "Japanese men are not supposed to go into the kitchen," replied my fiancée. "How often does your father go into the kitchen?" I asked. "Father has never been in the kitchen," came the reply.

> 1 pound potatoes
> 1 teaspoon sesame oil
> 2 teaspoons peanut oil
> 1/2 medium onion, minced
> Pinch of salt
> Pinch of freshly ground pepper
> Pinch of nutmeg

1 teaspoon Japanese curry paste,
     available at Japanese markets
2 ounces soft cream cheese
$^{1}/_{2}$ egg, beaten
14 ounces cooked sweet corn
$^{1}/_{2}$ cup flour
1 egg, beaten
2 cups *pan-ko* (Japanese bread crumbs)
8 cabbage leaves, thinly sliced

Boil the potatoes until soft. Drain and set aside. In a cast-iron skillet, sauté the onion in the sesame and peanut oils. Add the salt, pepper, nutmeg, and curry paste, and turn slowly in the pan for about 3 minutes, until the mixture is crumbly. Peel and mash potatoes, then mix potatoes and cream cheese in a large bowl.

Separate the cabbage leaves and soak in ice water. Set aside.

Divide the potato mixture to form 8 to 10 oval-shaped patties. Dredge each patty in the flour, then pat off the excess. Dip into the beaten egg, then coat with the *pan-ko* and place in the refrigerator for about 10 minutes.

Deep-fry the patties in 350 degree F oil for about 3 minutes on each side, until lightly browned. Drain on brown paper, then serve inside the cabbage leaves, after having splashed them lightly with *sanbaizu*—a mixture of equal parts soy, vinegar, and sugar.

Satoimo

Yuba Yaki

•

*Fried Satoimo
with Yuba in
Mushroom
Sauce*

Serves 4

• This recipe is comparatively rich, combining several of my favorite Japanese ingredients, and is also a bit *mendokusai* (troublesome) to make. It's a complete meal when eaten with cooked rice but is more notable for the use of *yuba*. *Yuba* is an intriguing by-product of the soybean. When soy milk is heated, a skin forms on the surface which is skimmed off and then can be hung out to dry in sheets. If dried, it keeps for a long time—one reason why it is such a favorite in China, where refrigeration is still a luxury in certain parts.

THE VEGETABLE MIXTURE:

8 small *satoimo* (Japanese tubers, similar to taro root)
2 sheets fresh or dried *yuba*
6 ounces *shimeji* mushrooms (oyster mushrooms)
4 large fresh shiitake mushrooms
1 (3-ounce) bag enoki
Pinch of salt
1 teaspoon whole-bean soy sauce
1 teaspoon sake
2 tablespoons flour
1 tablespoon peanut oil

THE COOKING BROTH:

1 1/2 cups *dashi*
1 tablespoon light soy sauce
1 tablespoon sake
1 tablespoon mirin
1/2 teaspoon salt
2 tablespoons cornstarch mixed with 2 tablespoons cold water

THE GARNISH:

8 sprigs *mitsuba* (Japanese herb), minced

Peel the *satoimo*. Sprinkle with a touch of salt and allow them to sit for 5 minutes. Rinse them in cold water and drain. Slice the *yuba* lengthwise into 1-inch strips. (For dried *yuba,* reconstitute the sheets in a little water.) Combine the *shimeji*, shiitake, and enoki mushrooms.

Mix the 1 teaspoon soy and the 1 teaspoon sake and sprinkle onto the *satoimo*. Dredge the *satoimo* in the flour. In a cast-iron skillet, fry the *satoimo* in the peanut oil over medium heat for 3 to 4 minutes, or until they become slightly tender.

Combine the cooking broth ingredients in a pot and add the *yuba* and mushrooms. Cover and simmer for 15 minutes over low heat. Remove the pot from the heat and stir in the cornstarch mixture until broth thickens and begins to glisten slightly.

Add the *satoimo* to the pot and transfer to a large serving dish. Sprinkle with the *mitsuba* and serve immediately.

Mizuna
Erini

•

*Sautéed
Japanese
Greens with
Fried Tofu
and Chili*

Serves 4

• One of the most charming things about listening to a Japanese person speak English is the way they tend to fracture it. Keiko-san is legendary with the malaprop, and some of them are so unintentionally witty I wonder if she secretly plans them. On one occasion, we received return mail from a letter she sent to someone on Santa Monica Boulevard in Los Angeles. When I looked at the envelope, marked "Addressee Unknown," I saw that the letter had been addressed to Santa Monica Bluebird.

Another time we were driving though Michigan and came across a sign: Kalamazoo, 11 Miles. Immediately, her face brightened. "Oh," she said, "that's one of my favorite books. I read it when I was in high school." "What book is that?" I asked. "You know," she said impatiently, "the famous one about the brothers by Dostoevsky."

Here is a dish made with *mizuna,* a leafy Japanese green with a mild, sweet flavor. The name comes from *mizu* (water), and the stalks are long and crisp. You'll probably only find the vegetable in a Japanese market, but you can substitute either bok choy or the Chinese greens called *choi sam.*

1 pound *mizuna* (about 1 head)
8 ounces *abura-age* (deep-fried tofu)
2 cups *dashi*
6 tablespoons sake
2 teaspoons mirin
2 teaspoons salt
2 teaspoons light soy sauce
3 teaspoons corn oil
Dash of *shichimi* (seven-spice seasoning)

Wash the *mizuna* thoroughly and cut into 1 ¹/₂-inch pieces. Cut the *abura-age* into thin strips and boil rapidly in water for about 30 seconds to remove excess oil. Remove the *abura-age* from the water, drain, and pat dry.

In a mixing bowl, combine the *dashi,* sake, mirin, salt, and soy sauce.

Heat the oil in a cast-iron skillet over high heat until it smokes slightly. Add the *mizuna* and *abura-age* and sauté vigorously, about 1 minute. Add the *dashi* mixture, cooking about 2 minutes, or until the *mizuna* softens. Sprinkle with *shichimi* and serve.

Nasu
Shishito
Takenoko
Yaki

•

Eggplant,
Green
Pepper, and
Bamboo
Shoot Stir-Fry

Serves 4

• Ethnic foods long have been wildly popular with the Japanese. In any major Japanese city, from Tokyo to Kagoshima (Japan's southernmost city), one can find all the major food cuisines—French, Italian, Indian, and a number of others.

But *chuka-ryoriya* (Chinese restaurants) have a special place in the Japanese heart. These restaurants are marked with a rectangle dissected vertically by a straight line, the eminently recognizable character meaning "middle" for China, as in the "middle kingdom." They can be found in some big-city neighborhoods, in major train stations, or in the most unlikely locales.

This next recipe is adapted from a dish that normally contains ground pork, the all-purpose meat used in Chinese home cooking. Instead of pork, *takenoko* (bamboo shoot) is substituted. If you would like a richer-tasting dish, add some minced shiitake mushrooms in place of the bamboo shoots.

The Japanese would call this a Chinese dish, primarily because cornstarch is used as a thickening agent. The main ingredients, though—Japanese eggplant, *shishito,* and minced bamboo—are immutably Japanese, and are employed in rendering a dish that any Chinese could find delicious, but certainly unfamiliar.

THE SAUCE:

1 1/2 to 2 tablespoons miso, preferably light brown
2 tablespoons whole-bean soy sauce
3 tablespoons sake
1 to 2 teaspoons *toobanjan* (spicy bean paste),
    available at most Asian markets
1 teaspoon sugar
1/2 cup water

5 whole Japanese eggplants, preferably small
12 *shishito* (Japanese green peppers)
4 ounces fresh bamboo shoot
1 piece ginger, about 2 inches long, chopped
2 or 3 leeks, finely chopped
4 teaspoons sesame oil
8 teaspoons peanut oil
1 tablespoon corn oil
Pinch of salt
Pinch of white pepper
1 teaspoon cornstarch dissolved in 1 teaspoon cold water

Combine all the ingredients for the sauce and set aside.

Remove the stems from the eggplants, but do not peel. Cut the eggplants into bite-sized chunks, no more than 2 inches thick, and set aside. Cut the *shishito* crosswise into 1/2- to 3/4-inch pieces, rinse in cold water, and set aside. Wash and peel the bamboo, and parboil it. Remove the bamboo from the water and rinse in cold water. Mince the bamboo until the pieces resemble ground meat.

Heat the sesame and peanut oils in a cast-iron skillet until bubbling, making sure the oil doesn't smoke. Ideally, the temperature should be about 330 degrees F. Stir-fry the eggplant and *shishito* in the oil, about 2 to 3 minutes, or until most of the oil is absorbed and the vegetables are gently browned. Remove the vegetables from the skillet and set aside.

Heat the corn oil in a separate skillet or wok (I recommend using a wok). When the oil starts to sizzle, add the ginger, leeks, and minced bamboo shoot. Stir-fry for about 45 seconds; the mixture should not brown. Add the salt and pepper. Stir in the sauce and continue stir-frying over medium heat, until the liquid boils. Add the eggplant and *shishito*. Stir in the cornstarch mixture, continuing to cook until the vegetables glisten and the sauce is thickened. Serve immediately.

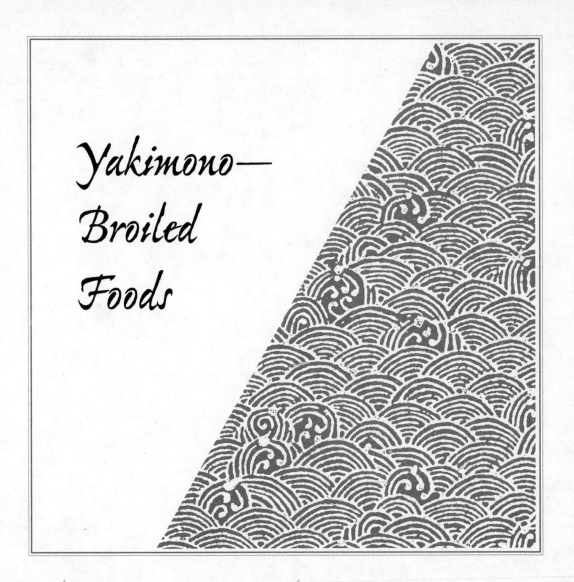

Yakimono—
Broiled
Foods

YAKIMONO IS A COMPLICATED notion in the Japanese kitchen, as the language makes no distinction between grilling and broiling. Consequently, foods cooked on a *hibachi* are considered *yakimono,* as well as foods broiled inside an oven. The Japanese greatly favor outside grilling over cooking in an oven. But because of the delicacy of certain fish, teriyaki—a sauce for fish (and not for chicken as it has been so corrupted in the West)—is typically made in the oven, as are a few *yakimono* where the sauce is baked into or on top of the dish.

Kaeru no ko
wa kaeru

The son of a
frog is a frog

•

*Baked
Eggplant
and
Assorted
Vegetables
with Miso
Paste*

Serves 2

• In this dish, a thick miso sauce bakes into the vegetables, forming a tasty brown crust. I use standard eggplant—rather than the longer, slender, and more flavorful Japanese variety—mainly for its visual effect.

THE MISO DRESSING:

4 tablespoons red or white miso
2/3 cup rice vinegar
4 tablespoons sugar
1 teaspoon *aji-no-moto* (MSG)

THE VEGETABLES:

1 eggplant
1 tablespoon corn oil
3 spears asparagus, halved and trimmed
1/4 cup chopped broccoli
1/4 cup chopped cauliflower
2 ounces fresh shiitake mushrooms, sliced

To make the miso dressing, combine the miso, rice vinegar, sugar, and *aji-no-moto* until the mixture is a smooth paste. Set aside.

Cut the eggplant in half lengthwise, and scoop out the flesh in the center. (Do not peel the eggplant, but leave a canoelike space in the center of each half.) Cut the eggplant flesh into 1-inch cubes. Sprinkle the eggplant halves lightly with salt, and allow them to sweat at least 10 minutes. Pat dry. In a cast-iron skillet, sauté the eggplant cubes in the corn oil over medium heat for 7 minutes, or until they are lightly browned. Drain the cubes on paper towels.

Bring a pot of water to a rapid boil. Add the broccoli, cauliflower, and asparagus and cook 3 to 4 minutes, until they soften slightly, but are not thoroughly cooked. Remove the vegetables from the pot, drain, and allow to cool slightly. Combine the vegetables with the eggplant cubes and most of the miso dressing. Save a bit of the dressing to put on top of the eggplant halves before they are placed in the oven.

Preheat the oven to 300 degrees F. Meanwhile, fill each eggplant cavity with a portion of the vegetable mixture, arranging the asparagus spears so that they jut out from the ends. Place equal portions of the shiitake mushrooms on top of each eggplant half.

Bake on foil or in a baking pan for 10 to 15 minutes, or until nicely browned. Serve immediately.

Nasu
Kyabetsu
Horensu
Yaki

•

Grilled
Eggplant
with Cabbage
and Spinach

Serves 4

• This dish uses Japanese eggplant, the undisputed star of the vegetarian grill. It's also a great dish to have with beer. Some people like heated sake with their Japanese dishes; others prefer beer; and still others, tea. I like beer because it neutralizes the acidity in ginger, which is a critical component of this dish.

8 Japanese eggplants
2 tablespoons corn or canola oil
6 large napa cabbage leaves
1 large bunch spinach
1 1/2 tablespoons whole-bean soy sauce
1 1/2 tablespoons ginger juice (squeezed out of grated fresh ginger)
1 tablespoon grated fresh ginger

Pierce the eggplants with a thin skewer in a few places and brush them lightly with the oil. Grill the eggplants over a charcoal fire or on a *hibachi* until the skins are charred and blackened evenly all over. Remove them from the fire, and place the eggplants in a brown paper bag and close tightly. Allow them to steam for a minute or two, then remove them from the bag. Pull off the skins in pieces, allowing some of the blackness to remain on the flesh of the eggplant.

Wash the cabbage and spinach. Remove the stems from the spinach. Bring a pot of lightly salted water to a boil. Plunge the cabbage leaves in the boiling water for a brief moment, until the leaves start to change color and go slightly limp. Remove the cabbage and plunge it into a bowl of ice water, stirring to cool quickly and preserve the color. Remove the cabbage from the water and drain. Repeat this process for the spinach.

Beat the fatter ends of the cabbage with the back of a flat-bladed knife to soften the leaves. Place the cabbage leaves, one overlapping another, on a *makisu* (bamboo rolling mat) with the thicker ends of each leaf at an outer end of the mat. Place the spinach on top of the cabbage, starting about 1 inch from the edge closest to you. Using the mat, roll into a cylinder, then remove the bamboo mat. Cut the vegetable roll into ¾-inch disks.

Into the bottoms of each of 4 small bowls, lay 2 or 3 slices of the cabbage rolls, angling them one atop another for visual effect. Lay 2 eggplants on top. Sprinkle with the soy sauce and ginger juice, and garnish with small pieces of grated ginger to taste.

Shiitake Shiso Yaki

•

Shiitake
Mushroom
Terrine
Seasoned
with Shiso
and a Spicy
Lotus Root
and Radish
Salad

Serves 4

• This slightly more creative—and more demanding—recipe from Pinot Bistro's Octavio Becerra, is one that requires an eye for color and a steady hand. Shiitake mushrooms have a penetrating flavor, which is one reason they are the main component in a good *dashi*. In this dish, the mushrooms harmonize skillfully with the eggplant and the mixture of oils, resulting in a complex, nutlike flavor.

A few of the ingredients, such as icicle radish and *kaiware* (daikon sprouts) may not be available outside specialty markets. Consult the list at the back of the book for the nearest Japanese market, bearing in mind that Japanese produce is always seasonal. This is a great summer and fall dish.

THE SHIITAKE MUSHROOM TERRINE:

2 large daikon radishes, thinly sliced
2 pounds large fresh shiitake mushrooms, stemmed
4 tablespoons cold unsalted butter
3 Japanese eggplant, thinly sliced lengthwise
1/2 ounce *shiso* (Japanese basil) leaves
Handful of sliced Japanese chives
1/2 cup grapeseed oil
1 lotus root, peeled and thinly sliced
1/2 bunch icicle radish
1/2 bunch butter sprouts
1 (2-ounce) package *kaiware* (daikon radish sprouts)
2 ounces julienned daikon radish
4 ounces pickled shallot rings
1/4 cup sesame oil
Shichimi (seven-spice seasoning) to taste

Preheat the oven to 325 degrees F. Briefly blanch the sliced daikon radish, and place it in a bowl of ice water to stop the cooking process. Line a rectangular terrine with plastic wrap. Drain the daikon radish thoroughly, and line the terrine with radish.

Place the shiitake mushrooms on a baking pan and place a touch of the cold butter onto each mushroom cap. Roast the shiitake mushrooms for 10 to 12 minutes, until they get a nice, golden brown finish. Set aside.

Season the eggplant with salt, pepper, and a little grapeseed oil. Place the eggplant onto a baking pan and roast for about 20 minutes, or until tender. Scrape the tender meat from the eggplant skin.

Line the terrine with a layer of the roasted shiitake mushrooms, a layer of the roasted Japanese eggplant, and then a layer of the whole *shiso* leaves. Alternate the layers until the terrine is almost full, and cover the top with plastic wrap. Allow to chill for about 24 hours, until firm.

In a blender, blend the chives and the grapeseed oil until an intensely green color and a nice smooth consistency is achieved. Set aside.

Peel and thinly slice the lotus root, then blanch. Combine the lotus root slices with the icicle radish, butter sprouts, *kaiware,* and julienned daikon radish. Season with the sesame oil and *shichimi.*

Unmold the terrine and slice it into $1/2$-inch slices. Place the slices in the center of an ornamental serving platter or round Japanese ceramic dish. Drizzle a touch of the chive oil on the terrine slices and the platter. Garnish with the spicy lotus root and radish salad, and top with the pickled shallots.

Ekkushen-
terikku
Nasu
Yaki

•

Grilled
Japanese
Eggplant
with
Vegetable
Dressing

Serves 6

• This recipe might seem slightly wacky to some people because of the banana. But the banana balances the strong flavors of the other ingredients and acts mostly as a thickening agent, much in the way it does in a fruit smoothie. And here's your chance to use a *hibachi,* the portable, pint-sized charcoal grill that caught on big during the sixties.

The idea for this dish was inspired by watching Japanese cable TV in Los Angeles. On the Japanese cooking shows, famous chefs square off against each other after being introduced with smoke and mirrors, the way Michael Jackson is at one of his concerts. The whole spectacle is then judged by a panel of three or four serious-looking *gurume* (gourmets). It's one of the funniest things I've ever seen on television, but guess what: These guys really know how to cook.

6 Japanese eggplants
2 tablespoons whole-bean soy sauce
$1/2$ banana
1 carrot, diced
$1/2$ medium tomato, seeds removed
$1/4$ cup minced onion
3 tablespoons rice vinegar
5 tablespoons corn oil
Pinch of salt
Pinch of *shichimi* (seven-spice seasoning)
Handful of *kaiware* (daikon radish sprouts)

Rinse the eggplants in cold water. Using a *hibachi* or gas or charcoal grill, cook the eggplants until the outside skin is thoroughly charred. Remove them from the grill and put them inside a brown paper bag and close tightly. After about 2 minutes, take the eggplants out of the bag, and pull their skins off. Sprinkle them with 1 tablespoon of the soy sauce and chill in the refrigerator for 1 hour.

In a blender, purée the banana with the carrot, tomato, and onion. With the blender running, add the rice vinegar and then the oil, drop by drop, until the mixture is thickened. Then add the remaining 1 tablespoon soy sauce, salt, and *shichimi*.

Put a portion of the banana mixture on six individual salad plates and spread it out so that each plate is covered. Place an eggplant atop each plate. Garnish with a few *kaiware* and serve.

Sunakku—

Snacks

*T*HE JAPANESE ALWAYS SEEM to be eating, whether the *senbei* (rice crackers), peanuts, and fried peas known as *otsumame* that businesspeople nibble in local pubs, the tempting rice triangles known as *onigiri* that are eaten anywhere from baseball stadiums to train stations, or the flavorful pancakes known as *okonomiyaki*, which are especially good in the Kansai area, from Osaka to Hiroshima.

Eating a series of small meals, rather than fewer large repasts as we tend to in the West, is a healthful choice. The Japanese propensity for this is one of the reasons that they control their weight so well, along with the relatively small amount of fat and protein in their traditional diet.

Hana yori dango

Dumplings
are better
than flowers

• Meaning "made to your choice—fried," *okonomiyaki* are the crepes, hotcakes, and waffles of Japan. In certain cities, you'll see people eating them with chopsticks, standing up at outside stalls, even in the dead of winter. This recipe follows the most common form: a pancake stuffed with spiced noodles and shredded vegetables. And any self-respecting Japanese would not recognize the taste if it did not include *okonomiyaki* sauce, a thick Worcestershire-sauce-like liquid available at most Japanese markets. (Try the one made by Otafuku, the Heinz of Japan.)

Theoretically, one could make *okonomiyaki* using any type of pancake flour, from buckwheat to buttermilk. I even have used Bisquick, but that doesn't strike me as very Japanese. The large areas afforded by griddles offer superior cooking for the pancake and filling, which need to be fried separately.

This traditional filling, which is cabbage and buckwheat flour noodles, often contains meat or fish in Japan, and almost always egg. The dish is made this way in Hiroshima, the most famous city in Japan for *okonomiyaki,* but I've omitted the sliced pork and *aji-no-moto* (MSG). Street stalls serving these pancakes in Japan add a pinch of MSG to the pancake batter. How authentic you want to be is a personal decision.

1 cup flour
1 1/2 cups water
1 teaspoon sugar
Pinch of salt
2 tablespoons corn oil
1 cup shredded *hakusai* (napa cabbage)
1/4 cup bean sprouts
Okonomiyaki sauce to taste
1/2 cup *Yakisoba* (see recipe)
1 egg
Shichimi (seven-spice seasoning) to taste
1 ounce pickled red ginger (optional)

Combine the flour, water, sugar, and salt, mixing well so that there are as few lumps as possible.

Add the oil to a hot cast-iron skillet, and using the back of a large metal spoon, slowly drop the batter onto the skillet in four 8-inch circles and fry over low to medium heat for 5 to 7 minutes, until the bottom of the pancakes are a rich, deep brown.

While the pancakes are cooking, lightly sauté the *hakusai* and bean sprouts in the same skillet, if there is room. Place portions of the *hakusai* mixture on top of the cooked pancakes and add a dash of the *okonomiyaki* sauce. Put the *yakisoba* on top of the cabbage mixture. Turn the pancake over using one or two spatulas. The noodles now are on the bottom, the vegetables in the middle, and the pancake on top. Cook for 2 to 3 minutes over low to medium heat.

In a separate skillet, fry an egg in a bit of oil, breaking the yolk and spreading it around on top of the white as it cooks. Place the pancake on top of the egg, pancake-side up, allowing everything to cook for about another 2 minutes.

Transfer the pancake egg-side up to a large plate. Brush the pancake with *okonomiyaki* sauce and sprinkle with *shichimi*. Serve with the pickled red ginger.

• *Onigiri* are often compared to sandwiches and are about as ubiquitous in Japan. Japanese literary references to them date back to the eleventh century, and in terms of Japan's population today, 135 million hungry people can't be wrong. You can buy these snacks in any convenience store throughout Japan, generally wrapped up in a stale, rubbery piece of *nori* and stuffed with one lonely looking shred of salted salmon, an *umeboshi*, or perhaps some *shiso* (Japanese basil). One of the best things about *onigiri* are their portability; they'll go anywhere—in a lunch box, pocket, or purse. And they are a truly casual food. In Japan, it is bad manners to eat as you walk down the street, but if what you are eating is *onigiri*, society is more understanding.

Make *onigiri* at home and they'll be a lot better than the ones you buy ready-made in stores. My favorite ones are *yaki-onigiri*, meaning toasted over an open flame. Certain pubs sell them this way, even though they are a bother to make and a rather low-profit item. (To toast *onigiri* at home, use a *hibachi*. Turn them over as the rice becomes golden; do not allow the rice to blacken.) *Onigiri* are great for picnics and afternoon snacks, and what's more, they're entirely nonfat.

12 ounces cooked Japanese rice
   (3 cups uncooked)
4 *umeboshi* (salted, pickled apricots), pitted
2 tablespoons black sesame seeds
1 sheet *nori*

Divide the rice into four equal parts, and then divide each part in half. Take a clump of rice into your palm and pat down, placing one of the *umeboshi* in the center. Now cover the clump with a second clump of rice and roll into a ball. Place the ball down on a flat surface, and shape it into a triangle. Repeat the process until four rice triangles are made.

Cover 2 of the triangles with black sesame seeds on both sides. Cut the *nori* in half. Wrap the other 2 with the *nori* around the base of the triangle, leaving some bare rice at the point. The triangles are now ready to eat or to be wrapped in plastic wrap for transport.

Makizushi

*Deep-Fried
Rice Rolls*

Serves 4

● When I was a student at the University of Wisconsin, a fish market on University Avenue served something that approximated these deep-fried rice rolls, mostly to please the vegetarian and organic eaters on campus. They were certainly the very first Japanese-style dish I ever tasted, and the first time I got to eat *nori*, even though I had no idea what it was at the time. (Had I known, I probably never would have eaten it in the first place.)

4 dried shiitake mushrooms
1 cup *dashi*
3 tablespoons sugar
2 tablespoons whole-bean soy sauce
2 ounces carrot, parboiled and cut into thin spears
2 ounces cooked *takenoko* (young bamboo shoot),
     cut into thin spears
2 eggs
1 teaspoon salt
4 cups Sushi Rice (page 133)
4 sheets *nori*
8 spinach leaves
3/4 cup peanut oil

Soak the mushrooms in cold water for 30 minutes and cut them into long, narrow strips about the size of the carrot and bamboo shoot spears. Place the *dashi* in a pot and add the sugar, soy sauce, and shiitake mushrooms. Bring to a boil and cook for 12 minutes. Add the carrot and bamboo shoot and cook over low heat for about 1 minute. Remove the vegetables from the heat and discard the liquid.

Make an omelet out of the eggs and the salt, then cut it into thin strips.

Divide the sushi rice into 4 equal parts. Place a sheet of *nori* on a *makisu* (bamboo rolling mat). Place a portion of rice on top of the *nori,* spreading it out evenly. Put equal portions of the egg, bamboo shoot, carrot, shiitake mushrooms, and spinach leaves on top of the rice, distributing them as evenly as possible. Using the mat, roll up the nori evenly. Pinch the ends together with a little water, if necessary. Repeat the procedure for the other 3 rolls.

Heat the peanut oil in a deep fryer and fry each roll separately, until the outside begins to brown nicely. Serve with a soy dipping sauce, and eat with *shoga* (pickled red ginger), which is available at any Japanese market.

• Nearly every Asian country has its own version of spring rolls: the dense bean-thread-noodle and crab imperial rolls of Vietnam; the tiny cylinders of ground beef Indonesians and Filipinos call *lumpia* and eat with peanut sauce; the Thai *poh pia;* and the original Chinese egg rolls themselves, which appear in dozens of incarnations.

Only the Japanese version of the spring roll, poetically named *harumake,* is traditionally vegetarian. Japanese people eat spring rolls mainly during the spring, but they make a delicious treat year-round. There are many ways to make them, but I prefer a simple version with cabbage, bean sprouts, bamboo shoots, shiitake, and julienned carrot. Eat them with a light soy dipping sauce containing some *momiji oroshi* (grated carrot). The wonton skins are available at most large urban supermarkets.

4 dried shiitake mushrooms
1/3 cup fresh bean sprouts
1 carrot
1/4 cup finely chopped cabbage
2 tablespoons sesame oil
2 tablespoons mirin
2 tablespoons dark soy sauce
pinch salt
10 Chinese egg roll skins
corn oil

Cut the shiitake mushrooms into thin strips and set them in a dish of cold water to reconstitute, about 20 minutes. Drain them and pat dry.

Rinse the bean sprouts and grate the carrot.

Heat the sesame oil in a cast-iron skillet. Add the carrot, shiitake mushrooms, cabbage, and bean sprouts, and sauté until tender, about 3 to 4 minutes. If the flavor of sesame oil is too strong you can use a lighter oil such as corn or safflower.

Remove the skillet from the heat. Add the mirin, soy sauce, and salt to the vegetables and mix thoroughly. Divide the vegetable mixture into 10 equal portions.

Take an egg roll skin, which is perfectly square, and lay it diagonally on a flat surface, diamond style. Place a portion of the vegetable mixture just above the bottom corner, then pick up that corner and fold it directly over the mixture. Do the same thing with the left and right corners. Now roll the skin upward into a cylinder and secure any loose flaps by patting them down with a little water.

Heat the corn oil in a deep fryer, wok, or large saucepan. Deep-fry the spring rolls until golden brown. Drain them on brown paper before serving.

• In the West we don't commonly associate asparagus with Japanese cooking, but in fact it is very popular in Japan. Available in green groceries throughout the country, asparagus is prepared in a variety of ways: skewered, breaded in the cooking style known as *kushikatsu,* as tempura, and as the snack we offer here. Because the Japanese are great bird-watchers, my Japanese friends love the etymology of the English name for this vegetable, derived from the Old English "sparrow grass." The sparrow, *sugumi* in Japanese, is a symbol of both piety and luck.

2 tablespoons yellow miso
8 ounces asparagus (about 10 to 12 stalks)
pinch salt
1 tablespoon mirin
1 tablespoon light soy sauce

Remove the yellow miso from the refrigerator and set out to bring to room temperature. This will bring out its flavor. Rinse the asparagus in ice water to remove any sand or grit, then cut off the tips.

Fill a saucepan with enough water to cover the asparagus, add the salt, and bring to a boil over high heat. Place the asparagus in the pan and cook until the spears are tender, 8 to 10 minutes.

Place the asparagus on a serving platter. Mix the mirin and light soy sauce, and pour the mixture over the spears. Spoon the yellow miso over the dish and serve.

Sushi—
For
Vegetarians

ONTRARY TO WHAT MOST people believe, sushi is not something made from raw fish, but rather is a generic term to describe bite-sized snacks made with a base of vinegared cooked rice. As a restaurant critic in Los Angeles, arguably the sushi capital of the Western world, I am always somewhat distressed because virtually everyone I know thinks that sushi is synonymous with Japanese food and vice versa. The truth is quite different.

When I lived in Japan, little stands sold sushi on street corners, but oddly enough, rarely sushi with fish. Fish is expensive, and as a filling snack, impractical. So a lot of the cheap and tasty sushi I first ate while in Japan as a student was filled with cucumber or carrot—really simple stuff.

Today, a vegetarian can be far more ambitious in the sushi world, even in Japan. The avocado of California roll fame has crept into the Japanese consciousness, and sushi variations from all over the world are beginning to appear in the more adventurous big-city *sushi-ya* (sushi restaurants).

The one thing that you will not see, just yet, is the rise of the female sushi chef. Japan has changed its attitudes greatly regarding women's issues in the last decade, but many Japanese chefs and gourmets have used the following excuse to keep women in front of, rather than behind, the sushi counter: "Women's cycles affect the way the rice tastes," they say, and that, for now, appears to be the end of the argument.

Sushi has become so popular where I live that any five-year-old in Southern California can probably name his three favorites . . . in Japanese. My Japanese friends in Los Angeles can't seem to get over the idea of Americans picking up boxes of ready-made sushi on their way home from work, but sushi and Southern California are so perfectly suited to one another that it was bound to happen.

Sushi in LA is a way of life. In upscale American supermarkets such as Gelson's in Encino or Bristol Farms in Pasadena, one can watch the sushi-makers plying their trade behind giant glass counters. Customers stop by to pick up a box of California roll for an afternoon snack. And because it is economical and easy to prepare, sushi has shown up on city school lunch menus. Neighborhood sushi bars are everywhere—hangouts with regular customers who have their own monogrammed *masuzake* (wooden sake boxes) stacked up along a back wall. Get yourself invited to a "wrap party," the traditional party a studio throws when a movie is finished, and it is a good bet that industry caterers have put together a giant tray of *tekkamaki* (tuna rolls) for the cast and crew.

Nowadays, superstar chefs all over the country are preparing creative vegetarian sushis that no Japanese in Japan would ever dream of eating. Many nutritionists, however, hype the benefits of this low-calorie snack, the efficiency of raw protein, the B-vitamins in rice, even the therapeutic effects of fresh ginger.

The sushi experience in the U.S. is very different from Japan's. To begin with, the atmosphere of the sushi bar in this country bears little similarity to the original. The more traditional sushi bars of Tokyo often are found in old houses, rather than being vehicles for modern architects done up in pink, gray, and pastels. We mix up the *wasabi* (green horseradish) in the soy sauce; they do not. Here, everyone at sushi bars talks to one another as if they are old friends, even though they may be total strangers; there, a sushi meal is generally quiet and contemplative, or a way for old friends to get together. And rarely would a Japanese wait in line for a seat at a sushi bar. He would simply go somewhere else.

Furthermore, many of the most popular sushi dishes in California and the rest of the U.S. just have begun to surface in Japan. California roll, a *makizushi* with crab and avocado, is one example. Another is a handroll that is eaten like an ice-cream cone, inside a wrapper of *nori*. I've included a few creative handrolls here, the handiwork of a couple of innovative young chefs.

The hands-down most famous sushi-maker in the U.S. right now is Nobu Matsuhisa, a wonderful creator. His restaurants, Matsuhisa, on Los Angeles' La Cienega Boulevard, and also Nobu, in Manhattan's SoHo, which he owns with actor Robert De Niro, are two of America's hottest restaurants at the moment.

If you're in Tokyo, try the sushi at Takeno, the famous restaurant in the fish market at Tsukiji or the extraordinary—and extraordinarily expensive—Kizushi. Takeno serves the freshest sushi on the planet. Kizushi will give you the chance to experience the work of Yamaguchi-san, one of Japan's master sushi-makers.

- 2 cups Japanese rice
- 2 cups water
- 1/4 cup mirin
- 1/4 ounce dried *kombu*
- 1/4 cup rice vinegar
- Pinch of sugar
- Pinch of salt

Thoroughly wash and drain the rice. Place the water, mirin, and *kombu* in a pot and bring to a boil. When the water comes to a boil, take out the *kombu* and add the rice. Cook for 20 to 25 minutes. Allow the rice to cool and transfer to a mixing bowl. Mix in the rice vinegar, sugar, and salt with a wooden paddle. If you like your sushi sweet, as they do in Kansai, add more sugar.

Maki
Rolls with
Pickled
Mango and
Carrot and
a Spicy
Asian
Vinaigrette

•

Serves 4

• The enigmatic Charlie Trotter just may be America's most brilliant young chef. He has helped transform Chicago into one of the country's most sophisti-cated dining towns with his restaurant, Charlie Trotter. Most critics hailed his Las Vegas restaurant, Charlie Trotter in the MGM Grand Hotel, as that city's very best dining spot before it recently closed. There, he served a vegetarian menu, and the food was spectacular. This is a variation of one of his recipes. It may be more complicated than most vegetarian sushi creations, but it is well worth the effort.

1 carrot, peeled and cut into $^1/_4$-inch sticks
1 small mango, peeled, pitted, and cut into $^1/_4$-inch sticks
1 teaspoon *wasabi* powder
3 tablespoons water
2 cups cooked Sushi Rice (page 133)
$^1/_4$ cup rice vinegar
2 tablespoons sugar
4 sheets *nori*
$^1/_2$ cup opal basil
1 red bell pepper, seeds removed, and cut into $^1/_4$-inch sticks

PICKLING JUICE

$^1/_4$ cup sugar
1 tablespoon salt
$^1/_3$ cup rice vinegar
$^1/_3$ cup sake
$^1/_3$ cup water

SPICY ASIAN VINAIGRETTE

$^1/_4$ cup sesame oil
$^1/_4$ cup peanut oil
$^1/_2$ cup rice vinegar
1 clove garlic, finely chopped
2 tablespoons shichimi

Place the carrots and mango in a small bowl and cover with the pickling juice.
Allow to marinate for about 2 hours in the refrigerator. Remove the mango
and carrot from the pickling juice, drain, and set aside. In a small cup, blend
the *wasabi* powder with the water, stirring until a smooth paste is formed.

In a separate bowl, combine the sushi rice, rice vinegar, and sugar, and stir
gently until the ingredients are well mixed. Lay out a *makisu* (bamboo rolling
mat) and top with 1 of the sheets of *nori*. Spread a quarter of the rice mixture
flat over the *nori* using the hands, leaving a 2-inch border at the top of the *nori*.
(Charlie Trotter recommends moistening the hands with water each time before
handling the rice, to prevent sticking.)

Spoon 1 teaspoon of the *wasabi* paste on top of the rice mixture, and place
a few leaves of the basil in the center. Lay a few pieces of mango on top of the
basil. Repeat with the carrot and then the red bell pepper.

Using the rolling mat, carefully roll up the *nori*, and as you near the 2-inch
border along the top of the *nori*, moisten it with water and seal up the roll. The
roll should be firm and smooth. Repeat the process to make the other 3 rolls.
Set the rolls aside for 30 minutes. Slice and serve at room temperature with the
spicy Asian vinaigrette for dipping.

*Mad
Max '84
Vegetable
Roll*

•

*Makes
2 rolls,
serving 10*

• Octavio Becerra of Pinot Bistro in Studio City, California, is one of the brightest young chefs I've ever met. In addition to having worked with master chef Joachim Splichal of Patina in Los Angeles, Becerra has cooked in Spain and France, and has also been influenced by prominent Los Angeles Japanese chefs Nobu Matsuhisa and Tommy Harase.

Pinot Bistro is known mostly for homey, hearty French bistro dishes. But Becerra has been known to sneak a Japanese dish or two onto his weekly tasting menus, and something like this is always received with enthusiasm by Los Angelenos, a crowd used to Asian flavors.

The following dish is something Becerra created while at Max au Triangle in Beverly Hills. It's a spectacular effort, and Becerra's use of grapeseed oil in place of more traditional Japanese cooking oils is interesting. "Grapeseed oil," says Becerra, "is ideal because it is low in cholesterol and neutral in flavor— an oil which doesn't overwhelm the natural flavors of a dish, as an oil like sesame will."

    2 bunches spinach leaves, washed
    1 avocado, peeled and puréed
    1/4 cup grapeseed oil
    1/4 cup rice vinegar
    4 shallots, diced
    Handful of finely sliced chives
    1/2 pound wild rice, rinsed and cooked until tender
    1 avocado, peeled and sliced into eighths
    3 red bell peppers, roasted and cleaned
    2 (1-ounce) packages *kaiware* (daikon radish sprouts)
    Olive oil for seasoning
    2 ounces onion sprouts
    2 red onions, thinly sliced and fried

Briefly blanch the spinach and immediately shock in ice water. Once the spinach is very cold, squeeze the water out thoroughly.

On a *makisu* (bamboo rolling mat) or square of waxed paper, spread out the spinach into a small rectangle.

Season the avocado purée with the grapeseed oil, rice vinegar, shallots, and chives. Add the avocado mixture to the wild rice.

Place the wild rice mixture onto the bottom third of the spinach. Create a small channel in the center of the wild rice mixture. Place the sliced avocado, roasted red bell peppers, and daikon sprouts in the channel. Lightly cover with a little more of the wild rice mixture. Cover the length of the wild rice with a piece of plastic wrap and press down gently with your hands.

Purée the remaining red bell peppers and season with a touch of olive oil. Place a drizzle of the red bell pepper purée onto a plate and top with a touch of olive oil. Cut the wild rice roll at different angles and lengths, then place the pieces on the purée in the center of the serving plate. Garnish with the onion sprouts, *kaiware,* and fried onions.

Inarizushi

•

*Tofu Purses
Stuffed with
Rice*

*Makes 10
inarizushi,
serving 5*

• *Inari* are sold all over Japan. They can also be found in most Japanese markets and snack shops in the U.S., Australia, and anywhere else there is a Japanese community. These little snacks may be the most popular and commonplace of all conventional forms of sushi in Japan.

Japanese dogs and cats are not pampered as they are in the U.S., and they are lucky to get *nokori* (leftovers), usually rice or sushi rice. One of my favorite cross-cultural encounters occurred one day in the Little Tokyo section of Los Angeles, while I was feeding some leftover *inari* to a hungry stray kitten. As I bent over the kitty and watched her gobble up the last delicious bits of my *inari*, I called out to her in Japanese, saying "*neko neko,*" the Japanese word for cat. Suddenly I saw three long shadows, and looked up to see the faces of three astonished businessmen, formally dressed in natty gray suits. After a brief moment, one of the men asked me, with great hesitation, "Are you . . . Japanese?" "No, but the cat is," I replied to their amusement.

6 ounces firm tofu, cut into 10 slices and fried
$^{1}/_{2}$ cup *dashi*
Dash of mirin
$^{1}/_{8}$ cup whole-bean soy sauce
$^{1}/_{2}$ recipe Sushi Rice (page 133)

With a sharp knife, make a thin, long slit in the center of each tofu slice big enough to stuff in the rice filling. Combine the *dashi,* mirin, and soy sauce in a saucepan, and bring to a gentle boil. Add the tofu and simmer until all the liquid is absorbed into the tofu. Let cool.

When the tofu is cool, stuff each slice with enough rice so that it resembles a square bundle. (Pat the rice in slowly, so as not to break the skin of the tofu.) Pinch the ends closed and serve with the *tsukemono* (pickle) of your choice. If possible, consume these within a few hours of preparation, as they tend to quickly lose their flavor.

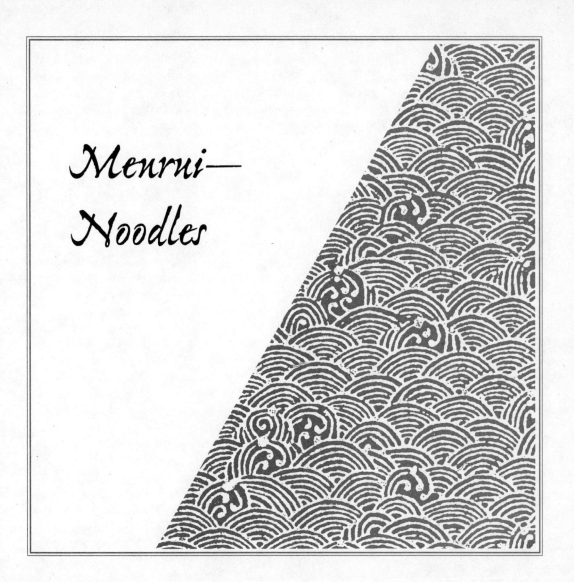

Menrui— Noodles

M ENRUI IS THE GENERIC Japanese term for noodles, whether they be the thick, wheat based *udon,* the delicate buckwheat noodles known as *soba,* the long wispy angel-hair-like *somen,* or garlicky *ramen* in broth. Perhaps no other people consume noodles with more fervor than the Japanese—not the Italians, not the Chinese. Metropolitan Tokyo, in fact, even has its own noodle museum, the Ramen Hakubutsukan, with eight noodle shops on the premises. Yet in Japan, which has more noodle restaurants per capita than any other country on earth, noodles are still not quite respectable. The Japanese eat them as a snack, and hardly ever as a main meal.

Here are some of the common noodle varieties and how they are served in Japanese restaurants:

Soba   buckwheat flour noodles, served in recipes that vary according to the season
Kitsune soba   *soba* with fried tofu and green onions in broth
Tenzaru   *soba* with tempura on the side
Tsukimi soba   *soba* with a raw egg on top in broth
Zarusoba   cold *soba* noodles with a side dish of dipping sauce, served in the summer for a refreshing lunch
Udon   noodles made of wheat flour, which are thicker than *soba* and most often cooked to a fairly soft texture. Like *soba,* they are usually served in a bowl with broth and toppings.
Kitsune udon   *udon* with fried tofu and green onions in broth
Nabeyaki udon   *udon* with vegetables and egg, which are cooked in an earthenware pot
Tempura udon   *udon* with tempura in broth
Ramen   spaghetti-like noodles served in a garlicky broth with a wide variety of toppings. It is the most popular noodle in Japan, often eaten in the wee hours after the bars are closed.

Wakame

Udon

•

*Thick
Noodles in
Soup with
Seaweed*

Serves 2

• *Udon* are the most filling and least expensive of the native Japanese noodlesthick, long, white tubes about twice as thick as bucatini, the fattest of the Italian pastas. It is possible to make *udon* yourself, but few home cooks would go to that kind of trouble.

Normally, one has to go to Japan to eat fresh *udon,* but a few small noodle houses in California, such as the Yoshimi Soba in Anaheim, makes noodles fresh on the premises. In his classic memoir *Between Meals,* journalist A. J. Liebling laments the modern scarcity of what he called "good little holes where you eat for nothing." Yoshimi Soba, and a few Little Tokyo noodle shops in Los Angeles such as Nanbantei, fit Liebling's description beautifully. Tokyo native Hiroshi Serizawa is the chef at Yoshimi Soba, and I have adapted two of his best dishes for this chapter. Serizawa recommends using Sanuki brand *udon,* which is made on the Japanese island Shikoku and is available frozen at many big-city Japanese markets.

5 cups water
8 ounces *udon*
2 ounces dried *wakame*
5 cups *dashi*
2 teaspoons whole-bean soy sauce
2 teaspoons salt
2 tablespoons chopped green onion

In a pot, bring the water to a boil and add the *udon*. Cook until tender, 1 to 2 minutes for fresh *udon* and 10 to 15 minutes for frozen *udon*. Do not overcook; *udon* should be chewy, with a nice bite. Drain the noodles in a colander and rinse them thoroughly with cold water, tossing gently. In a separate bowl, rinse the *wakame* with cold water to remove any salt. Drop the *wakame* in boiling water to quickly parboil, about 30 seconds. Drain the *wakame* in colander and set aside.

Simmer the *dashi,* soy sauce, and salt in a large pot until just below the boiling point. Before serving, reheat the *udon* for 20 seconds in boiling water and the *wakame* for 10 seconds, separately. Drain both again completely and place *udon* in a serving bowl, with the *wakame* on top. Pour in the *dashi* and garnish with the green onion. For a spicy addition, sprinkle liberally with *shichimi.*

*Buckwheat
Noodles in
Soup with
Grated
Mountain
Potato*

Serves 2

• This recipe also comes from Chef Serizawa. He insists on using homemade *soba* and wouldn't be caught dead cooking with any of the commercial brands. But any commercial brand will do, especially *sarashina,* a pure white soba made from the inside portion of the buckwheat kernel.

Tororo is a texture as well as a taste, best described by the colorful, onomatopoetic Japanese word *doro-doro,* literally translated as slimy. *Doro-doro* foods*natto* (fermented soybean) being the most notorious example*are perhaps those that non-Japanese palates have the most difficult time adjusting to.

Just as an aside, these double words are one of the most endearing and interesting features of the Japanese language; there are hundreds of them, and they always seem to become fetishes for those foreigners learning Japanese. *Petcha-petcha,* for instance, is the sound of rain splashing on a windowpane, but is also used by a scolding mother to indicate that a child is improperly smacking his lips. *Zara-zara* is the sound a man makes when he is slurping noodles. One of my personal favorites is *guzu-guzu,* a word whose meaning is somewhere in between puttering around the house and downright procrastination.

5 cups water
1 teaspoon rice vinegar
3 ounces *yamaimo* (Japanese mountain yam)
7 teaspoons *dashi*
5 ounces *soba*
1 sheet *nori,* sliced
1 quail egg
1/2 ounce *wasabi*
1/2 cup soy sauce
.2 tablespoons thinly sliced green onion

Combine the water and vinegar in a bowl. Peel the *yamaimo* and soak in the vinegared water for about 15 minutes, then grate finely. Set aside. Put the *dashi* in a chilled bowl and place in the refrigerator.

Bring a large pot of water to boil and cook the *soba* for 6 to 8 minutes, until tender but not soft; the *soba* should not be tough or elastic. Drain the noodles in a colander and rinse them thoroughly in cold water, tossing gently.

Place the *soba* on a serving dish and garnish with the grated *yamaimo*, *nori*, and quail egg in its shell. The steam from the *soba* will partially cook the quail egg. When the egg is cracked and the mixture is tossed, the dish will have the slimy texture known as *doro-doro*. Mix the *wasabi* with the soy sauce to make a dipping sauce. Garnish with the green onion and serve with the dipping sauce.

• *Somen* are hard to find in Japanese city restaurants; they are simple to prepare and usually eaten in homes. Bought in the package, these noodles are highly brittle and the color of old piano keys. *Somen* are also the noodles Japanese eat obsessively during the summer, the ones slurped with gusto from soy-flavored broth in iced-down bowls. "*Somen*," Japanese are fond of saying, "make you cool." Most Asian markets sell them in easy-to-cook bundles. Here is a simple suggestion for a refreshing summer snack.

1 (8-ounce) package *somen*
2 cups *dashi*
$^1/_8$ cup mirin
$^1/_8$ cup whole-bean soy sauce
2 tablespoons white sesame seeds
2 eggs
$^1/_4$ cup sugar
Pinch of salt
1 teaspoon corn oil
1 (4-ounce) bundle *kaiware* (daikon radish sprouts)
2 sheets *nori,* cut into thin strips
3 green onions, sliced

Boil the *somen* in a pot of water, making sure the noodles are thoroughly covered. Constantly separate the noodles so that they do not stick together. When the water froths and begins to reach the top of the pot, add $^{1}/_{2}$ cup ice-cold water. Cook for about 2 $^{1}/_{2}$ minutes more, until *al dente*. Remove the noodles from the pot, drain in a colander, and set aside.

To make a dipping sauce, combine the *dashi* with the mirin, soy sauce, and sesame seeds. Warm gently in a saucepan and set aside.

Beat the eggs, and stir in the sugar and salt. Fry the eggs in the corn oil in a Japanese omelet pan. Remove the eggs from the pan and cut into thin strips.

Place the dipping sauce into 2 small bowls. Place the *somen* in 2 bowls of ice water. Serve with the *kaiware*, eggs, *nori*, and green onions, arranging the toppings on a side plate as artfully as possible.

• For some reason, perhaps either speed or convenience, *ramen* have become the most popular form of Japanese noodles outside of Japan. But the Japanese themselves regard them as Chinese food. The middle character on the signs outside most *ramen-ya* (ramen shops) connote China, or more specifically Chinese food. In addition to serving a mind-numbing array of hot, garlicky soups, one can find fried noodles and lots of other Chinese treats on the menu.

In Japan, *ramen* is most emphatically a masculine food. Because it is one of the rare foods that employ garlic in this cuisine, women shy away from it in their desire not to offend the menfolk. It is also something a man rarely, if ever, eats before a date. Japanese men consider these healthful noodles a strong food, and many of them avoid *ramen* unless they plan an evening at the pub, or at home by themselves.

These noodles are named after the *kitsune* (fox) who, rumor has it, is crazy about fried tofu. I've never been able to determine whether or not the story is true, but I can tell you that this dish makes a great quick snack.

4 (1-ounce) sheets *abura-age* (deep-fried tofu)
2 ounces *hakusai* (napa cabbage), chopped
1 cup water
4 tablespoons whole-bean soy sauce
2 tablespoons mirin
2 tablespoons sake
1 quart *dashi*
2 cloves garlic, finely minced
4 (3-ounce) packages unflavored instant *ramen*
Sprinkle of white sesame seeds

Scald the *abura-age* in boiling water for about 30 seconds to remove excess oil. Pat the *abura-age* dry and cut the sheets in half. Boil the *hakusai* for about 2 minutes until tender and set aside.

Combine the water, soy sauce, mirin, and sake in a saucepan. Add the *abura-age* and the *hakusai*. Simmer over low heat for 5 to 8 minutes.

In a separate pot, bring the *dashi* to a low boil, and add the garlic and the *ramen*. The water will stop boiling for about a minute, but then will return to a boil. Then slowly add the soy sauce mixture, and boil the noodles for about 2 minutes more, making sure the noodles do not become soft or mushy. Ladle into individual bowls, sprinkle with the sesame seeds, and serve.

O-Cha and O-Kashi— Tea and Sweets

ANY BELIEVE THAT the Japanese do not have desserts. This is just not true. Just head over to the nearest *cha-ya* (tea shop) and get an eyeful of the dazzling, artistic sweets eaten with tea.

Most people know that Japan is a nation of tea drinkers. Tea in Japan is drunk hot, often more than 175 degrees F when served. This is a problem for people like me who are *nekojita* (literally "cat's tongue"), meaning those who cannot stand their beverages too hot. But extreme heating brings out the flavor of the tea leaves, and unlike our Lipton or orange pekoe teas, Japanese teas are never served tepid. From the lowly *bancha* to *matcha,* the lofty powdered green tea that is whipped into a froth during the tea ceremony, Japanese tea comes to the table piping hot. The thick ceramic teacups are designed to keep heat in, with many having lids for just that purpose.

Tea appeared in Japan in the ninth century, arriving from China like so much else in their culture. At first, it was brought in powdered form, and this survives in the tea ceremony, where the frothy whisked green tea is drunk out of a huge bowl. Tea time is usually at the end of a meal, or mirroring the British, taken with sweets in the late afternoon. Many delightful teas are sold at Japanese and Asian markets: *genmai cha,* made from brown rice; *mugi cha,* a barley tea; *hojicha,* a roasted, low-caffeine tea; and various grades of the ubiquitous green tea. It always adds to the ritual if you pour the tea from a gorgeous ceramic pot into exquisite little cups. A warning: A Japanese tea set can be extraordinarily expensive.

Japanese sweets, in general, fall into two categories: *yogashi* (Western-style sweets) and *wagashi* (traditional Japanese sweets). In addition, many formal restaurants and casual family gatherings feature fresh fruit as a last, or sweet, course. Among my most refreshing memories from Japan are two lush ripe strawberries, or a pair of *budo* (purple Japanese grapes), or slices of persimmon or Mandarin orange after a meal.

Fruits are eaten seasonally, of course. In the fall, there are grapes and the flavorful *nashi,* the crispy apple-pears that have begun to appear in our markets during the nineties. The winter brings *mikan,* an addictively sweet tangerine. The spring is likely to produce strawberries; the summer, a plethora of fruits. My favorite summer fruit is *hakuto,* the white peach from Okayama prefecture. Even the best Japanese sweet cannot compare with nature's bounty.

Yogashi are sold all over Japan, where as many Western-style bakeries per capita can be found as in most European countries. One popular favorite is the light sponge cake from the Portuguese called *castera;* another is a rolled, multi-layered German egg cake known as *baumkuchen.*

The Japanese prize delicious French pastries such as the chestnut cream cake *monburan* and a huge variety of American-style pies. It's also interesting to note that the Japanese are great coffee drinkers. Most of the world's Blue Mountain coffee from Jamaica, which is considered by many to be the world's best coffee bean, is sold to Japanese coffee distributors. And it is often coffee, not tea, that is used to wash down Western-style sweets.

Most Japanese sweets are based on *an,* a paste made from azuki beans and sugar. The most exquisite *wagashi* are sold in Kyoto—delicate, artistically perfect fruit jellies, molded flowers made from sweet bean, frosted sweetmeats in the shapes of birds and animals, and various rice flour pastries with *an* fillings. These are tremendously difficult to make, and so I suggest that if you wish to end a meal with them, you buy them at a Japanese department store, which are in some big U.S. cities.

One other style of sweets that I decided to omit from this book is anything made with *mochi,* a sticky rice paste made by pounding the rice until the gluten comes out. *Mochi* is terrific grilled, in soups and in sweets, but is extremely time-consuming to make and also a hazard to eat. It's traditionally eaten as part of the New Year's menu, and occasionally, this leads to calamity. The sticky substance can be dangerous when eaten too quickly or by someone who has had too much to drink. It sticks to the throat, and some have literally choked to death on it.

So instead, I'm including three recipes for intelligent and very Japanese desserts, all of which are easy to make and a great way to finish a meal. All go with either tea or coffee, though I personally favor *hojicha* whenever I come to the end of a Japanese meal.

• Japanese people might not consider this a dessert, but a Westerner probably would. It's a sweet dish used to temper the saltiness of *o-setchi ryori*, the traditional Japanese New Year's menu. New Year is a four-day holiday in Japan and the only official time of year that Japanese women get a break from their cooking chores.

Foods to be eaten over the New Year's break are prepared in advance. *Kazunoko* (herring roe), *takenoko* (young bamboo shoots), *kuri kinton* (preserved chestnuts), *kuromame* (black beans), and this two-toned egg cake are typical. The New Otani Hotel and Gardens in Los Angeles has gone so far as to offer a Japanese New Year's brunch, featuring these and other dishes. *Nishiki tamago* is one of the most popular dishes on the buffet.

6 eggs
8 tablespoons sugar
Pinch of salt

Preheat the oven to 375 degrees F. Meanwhile, boil the eggs for 10 to 12 minutes, until they are completely hard. Separate the yolks from the whites. Using the back of a large wooden spoon, mash the yolks, then the whites separately, through a fine wire mesh sieve, so that you have finely discrete pieces.

Mix 5 tablespoons of the sugar and the pinch of salt into the egg yolks. Mix the remaining 3 tablespoons of the sugar into the whites. Spread the egg white mixture onto the bottom layer of a small, 5 × 10-inch loaf pan, and then spread the egg yolks on top of the whites. Cover the pan with foil and make two or three small holes in the top. Place the loaf pan in a larger pan with 2 to 3 inches of water.

Bake for 12 to 15 minutes. Cool and unmold, cutting the cake into narrow slices.

• This unusual dessert is just a clever way to candy fruit, with the lemon-lime soda as the crowning touch. The recipe is adapted from the kitchen of Kozo Terajima. A talented chef, Terajima once owned the wonderful Kappo Kyara restaurant in Los Angeles, which in its day was probably the city's best and most refined place for Japanese pub food. Green apples are ideal to use in this recipe; sweet apples, such as Red Delicious, are totally inappropriate.

1 (12-ounce) can lemon-lime soda
5 tart apples
1 1/2 cups sugar
4 cups water
1/2 cup lemon juice
1/3 cup cornstarch

THE SAUCE:

1 cup water
1/3 cup sugar
2 teaspoons lemon juice

Partially freeze the soda in ice trays. Peel the apples and core them. Slice the apples into rings about 1 inch thick. Toss them with the sugar and place in a plastic bag or inside a covered pot, and allow the apples to rest, about 3 days.

Boil the apples in the water and lemon juice for 5 to 7 minutes, until the apples soften. Remove the apples from the pot and plunge them into a bowl filled with ice water. Remove the apple slices individually and pat them dry. Dredge the apples in cornstarch and bring them to a boil once again in a fresh pot of water. Transfer the apples to a bowl of ice water. Remove the apples, drain, and arrange them on dishes.

To make the sauce, combine the water, sugar, and lemon juice in a saucepan and bring to a boil.

Remove the partially frozen soda from the ice trays and place in a bowl. Mash with a fork to make it slushy. Top the apple rings with the sauce, and finish the plates with a spoonful of soda slush.

*Ginger-Pear Ice
Cream*

*Makes
1 1/2 quarts*

• It was the nineteenth-century French gastronome Brillat-Savarin who said, in his landmark work entitled *The Physiology of Taste,* that ice cream is the most "perfect and wonderful of all desserts." I second the motion.

Pears and ginger are well-known to be an inspired combination, but when the pears are Japanese apple-pears and the ginger is candied, the ice cream definitely belongs on both sides of the Pacific Rim.

2 large *nashi* (Japanese apple-pears),
    about 8 to 10 ounces each
1 cup milk
2 ounces candied ginger, available in
    Chinese markets
2 cups heavy cream
1 vanilla bean, split and scraped
8 egg yolks
1/2 cup sugar
1/2 teaspoon powdered ginger

Peel and core the *nashi,* then purée them with about 1/8 cup of the milk until they are pulpy and slushy. Finely mince the ginger into tiny nuggets.

In a saucepan, heat the cream and the remaining milk with the vanilla bean, but do not boil. Cover the pan and remove from the heat. Let the mixture steep for up to 1 hour.

Beat the egg yolks and sugar together until the sugar has been absorbed thoroughly. Reheat the cream mixture over low heat until warm. Pour about 3/4 cup of the cream mixture into the egg yolks, whisking constantly. Add this egg mixture into the rest of the cream mixture, and then slowly beat in the puréed *nashi.* When the mixture is nice and thick, remove the pan from the heat, and stir in the candied ginger.

Freeze in an ice-cream machine according to the manufacturer's directions.

Japanese desserts are often filled with red paste made from nothing more than azuki beans and sugar. Dumplings called *chumanju* are made from wheat flour, and the paste is also used to stuff rice cakes, served in a jellied form, as an ice-cream topping and in a cold soup. For Westerners, it is an acquired taste, but most Asian peoples love it. Try smearing some on a piece of bread, the way we would do with peanut butter or marshmallow cream. It's high in protein and low in fat, a better nutritional balance than offered by the majority of our desserts.

1 cup azuki beans
1/2 cup sugar
pinch salt

In an uncovered pot, boil and drain the azuki beans in approximately 1 quart of water, adding cold water to the beans as the water boils off. The beans should be extremely soft in about 30–35 minutes. Keep the water the beans were boiled in when they are ready to work with.

Using a sieve or colander, smash the beans so that the skins remain behind, and then mix the residual paste up in the water. Using a fine sieve, remove any rough pieces or remaining skins. Further drain the mixture in an absorbent cloth, until it is slightly pasty.

One tablespoonful at a time, stir in the sugar, until the paste is thick and sweet. Refrigerate, and the paste will keep for quite a long time, to be used as a topping, in pastries, or as a spread. The paste is especially delicious on buttermilk pancakes, and will add an exotic touch to a Sunday brunch.

◆ Almost every Japanese restaurant catering to Westerners features both green tea and red bean ice creams on the menu. Cultivated for Western palates, these sweet dairy anomalies have filtered back to Japan—now they are more popular with the Japanese than with Westerners. Until the latter part of this century, the Japanese consumed little in the way of dairy products.

This most identifiably Japanese of all ice-cream flavors is a good example of how fusion in cuisine can influence the country of origin. Green tea ice cream is incredibly easy to make at home. I recommend doing so instead of buying the low-butterfat, insipid green tea ice creams manufactured en masse. But it isn't necessary to start from scratch. Do as I do, and use a premium brand of ice cream for a base.

> 3 to 4 teaspoons *matcha* (green tea)
> 1 hand-packed pint of Häagen-Dazs
>   vanilla ice cream, or your favorite brand

Dissolve the *matcha* in 3 to 4 teaspoons of scalding hot water, so that it forms a pasty green liquid.

In a food processor, combine the ice cream and the tea paste until they are thoroughly mixed. Do not let the ice cream soften too much. Divide the ice cream equally into 3 or 4 bowls and set in the freezer to firm. Serve.

In order to best prepare Japanese recipes, you'll need to visit one of these markets. Certain Japanese vegetables like *kikuna, nira,* and *gobo* are mostly unobtainable in ordinary supermarkets, and besides, a trip to one of these markets is instructive and fun.

ALABAMA

Ebino Oriental Food and Carry Out

Montgomery   (205) 265-4001

CALIFORNIA

Aloha Grocery

Los Angeles   (213) 822-2288

Asahiya

Stockton   (209) 464-9341

Asia Food Market

Sacramento   (916) 366-6852

Berkeley Bowl

Berkeley   (510) 843-6929

Dobashi Market

San Jose   (408) 295-7794

Ebisu Oriental Market

Fountain Valley   (714) 962-2108

Eiko Market

Irvine   (714) 551-3200

Enbun Market

Los Angeles   (213) 680-3280

Hadaya Market

Pleasant Hill   (415) 676-5128

Han's Oriental Market

Marina   (408) 384-6741

Hinokuni

Sacramento   (916) 422-8849

Hiro Japanese Grocery

Fairfield   (707) 422-7266

Imahara Fresh Produce

Cupertino   (408) 257-5636

Marukai Wholesale Mart	**Spark**
Gardena (213) 538-4027	San Mateo (415) 571-8620
Maruwa Foods	**Sunrise Oriental Food and Gift Shop**
San Francisco (415) 563-1901	Carlsbad (619) 729-5888
Modern Food Market	**Super Koyama**
Los Angeles (213) 680-9595	San Francisco (415) 921-6529
Nak's Oriental Market	**Suruki Market**
Menlo Park (415) 325-2046	San Mateo (415) 347-5288
New Meiji Market	**Takahashi Shokai**
Gardena (213) 321-4734	San Mateo (415) 343-0394
Nijiya Market	**Tokyo Fish Market**
San Diego (619) 268-3821	Berkeley (510) 542-7243
Oriental Food Fair	**Tokyo Oriental Food**
El Cerrito (510) 526-7444	Salinas (408) 424-1175
Oto's Japan Food	**Tozai Foods Market**
Sacramento (916) 424-2398	San Gabriel (818) 288-5124
Senator Fish Market	**Uoki Sakai**
Sacramento (916) 443-5042	San Francisco (415) 921-0515
Senri Market	**Vista Oriental Market**
Monterey Park (818) 573-3860	Vista (619) 726-7216

Yamamoto Shoten

Vallejo   (707) 644-6099

Yaohan

Costa Mesa   (714) 557-6699

Yaohan

San Jose   (408) 255-6699

Yaohan

Torrance   (213) 516-6699

FLORIDA

Japanese Fish Market

Fort Lauderdale   (305) 772-0555

Nippan Daido USA, Inc.

Chamblee   (404) 455-3846

Oriental Market

Augusta   (404) 793-4249

Tokyo Food Market

Melbourne   (407) 254-9317

Tomiko Oriental Food and Gifts

Mary Esther   (904) 244-3022

ILLINOIS

Kishuya

Morton Grove   (708) 965-4774

Koyama Shoten

Mt. Prospect   (708) 228-5544

Shimada Shoten

Mt. Prospect   (708) 640-1222

LOUISIANA

Oriental Merchandise Co.

Metairie   (504) 888-3191

U.S. Japan Grocery

Metairie   (504) 831-7404

MARYLAND

Daruma Japanese Grocery

Rockville   (301) 881-6966

Lotte Oriental Supermarket

Rockville   (301) 881-3355

Sakura Books and Food

Rockville   (301) 468-0605

Japan Food Express

Las Vegas   (702) 737-0881

Kotobukiya

Cambridge   (617) 354-6914

Yoshinoya, Inc.

Cambridge   (617) 491-8221

Bellmart

Ridgewood   (201) 444-8752

Chang's Oriental Market

Fort Lee   (201) 944-9009

Nippan Daido USA, Inc.

Fort Lee   (201) 944-0020

Sakanaya

Fort Lee   (201) 224-0774

Yaohan/New York

Edgewater   (201) 941-9113

Koyama Shoten/Detroit

Livonia   (313) 464-1480

Noble Fish Market

Clawson   (313) 585-2314

Unagiya

Farmington Hills   (313) 855-1660

Hartsdale Meidiya

Hartsdale   (914) 949-2178

Katagiri and Co., Inc.

New York   (212) 755-3566

Meijiya Yonkers

Scarsdale   (914) 961-1257

Nippan Daido USA, Inc.

Flushing   (718) 961-1550

Nippan Daido USA, Inc.

White Plains   (914) 683-6735

Sam Bok Grocery

New York   (212) 582-4730

Shin Nippondo

Jamaica   (718) 380-4950

Shinsendo

Mamaroneck   (914) 698-5450

OHIO

(Dofi) Dayton Oriental Food

Dayton   (513) 254-3711

Koyama Shoten

Columbus   (614) 761-8118

Koyama Shoten

Dayton   (513) 275-9111

Noble Fish Co., Inc.

Cleveland   (216) 268-4433

OREGON

Anzen Import

Beaverton   (503) 627-0913

Anzen Import

Portland   (503) 233-5111

Asia Market

Corvallis   (503) 758-5366

SOUTH CAROLINA

Chieko Japanese Food Store

Columbia   (803) 788-1418

TEXAS

Asahi Imports, Inc.

Austin   (512) 453-1850

**Edoya Oriental Foods
and Gift Store**

Dallas   (214) 247-0393

Kazy's Gourmet Shop

Dallas   (214) 235-4831

Nippan Daido USA, Inc.

Houston   (713) 785-0815

UTAH

Sage Farm Market

Salt Lake City   (801) 484-4122

WASHINGTON

Fuji 10 Cent Store

Tacoma   (206) 474-5566

Sanshin, Inc.

Parkland   (206) 536-2261

Tacoma Tofu, Inc.

Tacoma   (206) 582-6816

Uwajimaya

Bellevue   (206) 747-9012

Uwajimaya

Seattle   (206) 624-6248

abura-age deep-fried tofu sold in sheets at Japanese markets
aemono mixed foods
agemono fried foods
aji-no-moto MSG
akamiso red paste made from fermented soy beans
an a dessert filling made from puréed azuki beans and sugar
aoshiso sweet basil

bento the Japanese lunch tray or box, usually compartmentalized and made of
    lacquered wood
budo grapes

castera light sponge cake of Portuguese origin
chawan tea bowl
chawan mushi steamed soy milk custard
cha-ya tea house
chuka-ryori Chinese restaurant

daibutsu giant, gilded statue of Buddha
dashi basic soup stock used as a base in most dishes
donabe Japanese earthenware pot
donburi a large serving bowl, often ceramic
doro-doro a slimy, slippery texture

ebi shrimp or prawns
Edo the old name for Tokyo before the reign of the Meiji emperor

furo bath

gammodoki deep-fried tofu burger made with puréed yams
gehin low-class
genmai brown rice
gingko a Japanese nut with a mild, bitter aftertaste
gobo burdock root

go don bento "five-drawers lunch box"
gohan rice
goma sesame seeds
gomadofu a sesame-based food with the consistency of tofu
guzu-guzu to putter around the house, to procrastinate
gyoza fried dumplings
gyoza-no-kawa gyoza wrappers

hade flashy
hakusai napa cabbage
harumaki spring rolls
hashi chopsticks
hibachi portable, pint-sized charcoal grill
hijiki a seaweed with a rich, black sheen
hitokuchi one mouthful
hocho knife
hojicha a roasted, low-caffeine tea, brown in color
horenso spinach

inari fried, rice-stuffed tofu snack
irasshaimase "welcome" or "please come in," usually shouted in sushi bars and
    Japanese pubs
itadakimasu "I'm eating," uttered before taking the first bite at a Japanese table
itamemono steam-sautéed foods
izakaya pub specializing in sake and small dishes

kabocha pumpkin
kakejiku scroll paintings
kakushiaji a "suspicion," or tiny, almost undetectable amount
kaiseki a multi-course meal, or a meal served with the tea ceremony
kaiware daikon radish sprouts
kamaboko colorful, oddly shaped cakes made from fish paste
kamameshi rice casserole

Kansai "west of the barrier," the region containing Kyoto, Osaka, and Kobe

Kanto "east of the barrier," the region containing Tokyo

karai spicy dishes

karashi very spicy powdered mustard that is mixed with water to form a paste

katakuikko Japanese potato starch

katsuobushi dried bonito flakes, primarily used to flavor stock or as a savory topping

kikuna the edible leaves of the chrysanthemum

kinnoko type of mushroom

kinugoshi silken-style tofu

kishimen flat, ribbonlike wheat noodles

kitsune fox

kobachi large bowls used for noodles

kombu kelp

konnyaku "devil's tongue," a rubbery yam cake often cut into squiggly strips

koroke croquette

kotatsu low table with a heating element underneath

kuppamaki a type of rolled sushi

kura black

kuragoma black sesame seeds

kuri kinton preserved chestnuts

kushi-katsu fried delicacies on skewers

kuzu a crumbly white substance from the *kuzu* plant used as a thickening agent

kyuuri cucumber

maki suffix meaning "roll"

makisu small mats of woven bamboo used for rolling sushi

makizushi sushi handroll

masuzake square cedar boxes, often monogrammed, for drinking sake

matcha powdered green tea whipped with water, which is served frothy, and used in the tea ceremony

matsutake the rarest and most costly of all Japanese mushrooms

Meiji the emperor who opened Japan to the West in the late nineteenth century
mendokusai troublesome
menrui the generic term for noodles
meshi meal
mikan Japanese tangerines
mirin sweetened rice wine used in cooking
miso fermented soy bean paste
misoshiro white miso used for making soup
mitsuba a pungent herb, which is a member of the basil family, known as
    trefoil in English—available in Japanese markets
mizu water
mizun leafy Japanese green with a mild, sweet flavor
mochi a pounded rice cake with a sticky, glutinous texture
momein "cotton" tofu
mushimono steamed foods
mushi-yukan a popular steamed sweet made from *an*, wheat flour, and
    chestnuts

nabe cooking pots in a variety of shapes
nabemono things cooked in the pot; one-dish meals
nasu Japanese eggplant
natto fermented soybean paste
nekojita "cat's tongue," or someone who can't stand hot things
nimono simmered foods
nira garlic chives
nokori leftovers
noren hanging, cloth curtains
nori dried laver, a type of sea plant, usually sold in crackly green sheets
norimaki cooked rice rolled inside a cylinder of nori

oden a stew made with vegetables, tofu, and other items, which are cut into
    geometrical shapes

okara a by-product of the soybean
okawari second helping
okazu side dish
okonomiyaki stuffed pancakes
o-mi-o-tsuke informal term for miso soup
onigiri savory, filled rice triangles
oroshi grated vegetable garnish
o-setchi-ryori Japanese New Year dishes, most of which keep several days
otoshi-buta a wooden, thick handled drop lid used in simmering
otsumame snacks eaten when drinking alcoholic beverages

pan-ko bread crumbs
petcha-petcha to smack the lips
ponzu a citrus-based flavoring or dipping sauce

ramen long, skinny wheat noodles, eaten in a garlicky broth
ramen-ya ramen shop
renkon lotus root
ryokan the most elegant category of traditional Japanese hostelry

saikyo miso white miso flavored with sake
sakaba a kind of pub, which derives its name from sake
sake Japanese rice wine
samurai medieval Japanese warrior
sanbaizu "three components," a sauce made from soy, sake, and vinegar
sansai "wild moutain," a term used to describe a cooking style or
    certain wild foods
sansho a powder made from the dried pod of the prickly ash plant
sarashina a delicate buckwheat flour
satoimo similar to taro, a starchy tuber
satsumaimo another sweeter type of tuber
seiza seated with the legs folded under

senbei rice crackers
sento public bathhouse
shamoji large wooden spoon used for serving rice
shichimi "seven flavors," a ground spice mixture
shimeji oyster mushroom
shiro white
shirogoma white sesame seeds
shishito Japanese green peppers
shiso the beefsteak plant, commonly refered to as Japanese basil
shitamachi downtown
shoga pickled red ginger
shoji sliding door screens
shojin-ryori an elaborate vegetarian cooking style, which began in
    Buddhist temples
shokudo cafeteria
soba buckwheat-flour noodles
somen long, spaghetti-like noodles, often consumed cold
sukiyaki nabe a heavy, long-handled cast-iron skillet
suimono water foods, mostly clear soups
sumiso a mixture of miso and vinegar
sunomono vinegared foods
suribachi mortar
sushi-ya sushi restaurant

tai red snapper
takenoko young bamboo shoots
takuan basic pickle made from daikon radish and fermented rice bran
tamagoyaki flaky rolled omelet
tatami straw mat
teishoku a set meal or complete dinner
tekkamaki tuna roll
tempura battered, fried vegetables or fish

teriyaki a well-known thick sweet sauce generally used in the preparation of fish
tokonoma raised placed of honor
toobanjam spicy bean paste from China
tororo a slimy, grated dish made from yam mixed with raw quail egg
tosto toast
tsukemono generic name for Japanese pickles
tsukimi "moon viewing," a name for a noodle dish

udon a thick wheat noodle
umeboshi pungent pickled fruit, more like apricots but often referred to as plums
usubabocho a flat-bladed carving knife

wa harmony
wagashi Japanese sweets, most of which contain beans and sugar
wakame an edible sea plant
waribashi wooden, throwaway chopsticks, often wrapped in paper
wasabi green horseradish, always eaten grated, or powdered and mixed
   with water

yakimono broiled foods. Also, fine Japanese pottery.
yakitori skewered broiled chicken
yamaimo "mountain potato," a kind of tuber
yatai outdoor food stall, or food tent
yogashi Western-style sweets popular in Japan
yojoohan a small room the size of $4\frac{1}{2}$ tatami mats
yuba dried sheets made from skimming the surface of boiling soy milk
yukata Japanese bathrobe, usually made of printed cotton
yuzu a Japanese citrus fruit with a medicinal taste

zabuton embroidered cushions
zara-zara the slurping sound made when noisily eating noodles
zensai appetizers